Bishops Lydeard Revisited

with
Cothelstone & Cotford

by
David J. Hinton

ISBN 18999520X

Printed in Great Britain by
Taunton Printing Company

Bishops Lydeard Revisited

with

Cothelstone & Cotford

Cover Pictures

Top, left to right: Lady Alianore Lethbridge, Alwyne and Phyllis Axe
Col. Boles, Dr Aveline.
Middle: Watts House c.1850.
Bottom, left to right: Edward Jeffries Esdaile, four generations of the Saunders
family, Mrs Florence Woollen.
Back Cover: Across Cothelstone Manor to Lydeard Hill.

Acknowledgements

The author would like to thank the following for their time and contributions in the compilation of this book. Sadly some of them are no longer with us and it is to be hoped that their words and pictures are a pleasant memory for their families and also the villagers who had the priviledge of knowing them:

*Phyllis Axe, Mary Bird, Nick Bucknall, Sir Jeremy Boles,
Fred Clarke, Minnie Eller, George Grimstone, Bill Hares,
Fiona and Geoff Kearns, Pat Lathbury, Margaret Morris,
Gladys Palmer, Don and Gwen Saunders, Ray Smith, Ernest Stephens, Jim Stutt,
Douglas Wade, Jane Warmington, Philip Woodgate-Jones,
Florence Woollen.*

Other Sources:
*The Esdaile Journal
Parish Council Minutes
Somerset Records Office
Somerset County Gazette.*

CONTENTS

Preface

The old rural world still survives in the memories of the men and women who lived and worked in our village during the first decades of the last century. Their lives, shaped by local custom and traditional ideas, seem closer to the 18th century than the new millennium. The aim of this book is to capture the stories of those people who can still recall the time-honoured rural way of life in Bishops Lydeard before it vanishes forever. The age of oxen and horsepower on the farm, when they pulled everything from ploughs to carts, has gone. The old village, once a bustling self-contained community, living off the land or the patronage of the Squire, has now largely become a middle-class enclave.

For generations, village life has been regarded as the epitome of our national character, forming a central place in our sense of history. There is a huge and growing nostalgia for popular histories and village photograph books, which paint a picture of our rural past. It is these images of a rural idyll which have fuelled the gentrification of villages by the middle classes.

However, there was a darker side. Exploitation by the landowners and farmers who paid very low wages, frequent absence of facilities such as running water and sanitation and the poverty of many who lived here. Despite these hardships it is hoped that the writings and words of the people in this book display a dignity, determination, good humour, creativity, resourcefulness and sheer hard graft often in the face of most difficult and demanding circumstances.

Documented in the book is the authentic voice of country people from the top to the bottom of the social scale. Featured are the written records of people who have lived in past centuries in this village and the collected stories of those who are now in the twilight of their years. It tells their stories, often in their own words and possibly for the first time. I hope I have done them justice and I thank them all.

David J Hinton
Piffins
Bishops Lydeard.
July 2004

Picture of the author courtesy of
Christopher Rimmer A.R.P.S.

Prologue

After the Norman Conquest, Bishops Lydeard was no exception in assimilating people from across the Channel over the next two centuries. In 1327 their names bear witness to this, Richardo le Knight, Johanne de Gavelbrig, Rogero le Fox and Johanne le Hore, for example. The poorer men in the village were identified by location: Nicholas at the Bridge, John by South Brook, William at the Street and William at the Wyche (wych tree).

Wool had become a profitable commodity, although it was not known how to make it into cloth unless of a very coarse kind, called friezes. Most of our wool was exported to the Netherlands. Edward III induced Flemish manufacturers to bring their art to England by offering a superior style of living, a share of profits and connections with the best families. Some Flemings had settled in and around Taunton by 1336. Serge cloths became their speciality.

The importance of wool to inhabitants in Bishops Lydeard is demonstrated through the will of John Smert, who died in 1422, who bequeathed a fleece of sheep's wool to each of his godsons, and he, for the time, was quite well off leaving 20 marks (£13.33) to his wife, Christina. The increased financial fortune of the village was manifested by the completion, in 1472, of the fine church tower and later the construction of a Guild Hall.

Over the next two centuries Bishops Lydeard prospered and the population

Guildhall and St Mary's Church, Bishops Lydeard.

increased, although for the poorest life continued to be governed by the slow, steady progression of spring, summer, autumn and winter. The passage from one season to another was marked by various festivals and ceremonies often pagan in origin.

The harvest was a special time marking the end of one growing cycle or the beginning of the next. It was time to give thanks for the year's crops safely in the barn - the winter's hardships could be faced with a degree of confidence. The cutting of the last sheaf was filled with significance, jubilation was tinged with a sense of foreboding. The man cutting the last sheaf was thought to be killing the corn spirit, which would bring him bad luck. So all the men would throw their sickles at the last sheaf so that there would be a shared responsibility, dividing the individual share of bad luck.

Once the corn was cut it had to be brought by oxen and cart to the barns and the completion of this task was the subject of great celebration. The harvest wagon was decorated with flowers to bring in the last load - a "Corn Dolly" often held aloft in triumph as it passed through the village. It became customary for a feast to be held for all who had taken part in bringing in the harvest - this was known as the "Harvest Supper" and would often include such treats as a goose, pork, beef, apple pies and plum pudding as well as plentiful supplies of cider. After the supper women and children were allowed to go and collect any left-over crops from the fields. This was known as "gleaning". The church bell was rung to signal the start and the whole process was strictly controlled.

By 1548 the old feudal Lordship of the Bishops of Wells was gone and wealthy individuals purchased the Manor.

The Old Market Cross 1656

Sir John Stawell 1600 - 1662

— One —
Tales from the Seventeenth Century

Misdemeanours

Turbulent Years - Sir John Stawell

The Stawell Family Arms

Tales from the Seventeenth Century

The importance of the village as a market town, by the 17th century, was marked by the erection of the market cross (at the entrance to Old Vicarage Lane and now in the churchyard). The new landowners began to act as benefactors to the village. The village street scene changed in 1616 with the construction of the almshouses built by the then landowner Sir Richard Grobham, (from Great Wishford in Wiltshire.) in memory of his father Sir Nicholas Grobham. Eight poor of Bishops Lydeard were housed and each had a small garden.

Misdemeanours

An increasing population brought with it a number of people who took a perverse delight in causing trouble for others. Nothing changes! In the Quarter Session records for Somerset are petitions that give an interesting insight into some of them.

Two of the biggest troublemakers in 1603 were Thomas Bird and Matthew Nation.

A list of the misdemeanours of Thomas Bird - a tailor.
'Now in the jail with request there to remain for examples sake.
Firstly the Constable of Lydeard Episcopi having peace process against him, Thomas Bird drew his knife and there would have stabbed both the constable and his son therewith if he had not thereof been prevented.
Secondly he is a common alehouse haunter and a most disordered person.
Thirdly he did beat Thomas Gunn, the 8th day of June 1603. He also beat Richard Pole's wife, on 27th August. He likewise assaulted the Constable and Tithingman on the same day 8th June and said he repented that he had not killed one or more of them.
Fourthly being presented at sundry Petty sessions in Wiveliscombe for sundry misdemeanours did give forth very lewd speeches not tolerable and threateneth to kill them who go about and attempt to bring him before the justices and he still continues his lewd life.
Signed by John Francis and Humphrey Wyndham.'

If you think that was bad, Matthew Nation was even worse.
'The wicked misdemeanours of Matthew Nation and great abuses done by him the which is very odious and bad and the great disliking of all the country. And has persevered in it continually more like a savage creature than a Christian. We most humbly petition entreating reformation of a better course of life and punishment according to his deserts: then they begin.

In premise (at first) the day before he was chosen tithingman he went to the house of Thomas Bird and there was in certain company a whole day and night and part of another day and was very much drunk and forgetfull of himself and a horn being winded in the house, as he lay on the ground he could not awake.

The 28th day of June last past the aforesaid Nation was drinking at a house and carousing and made some of his company drunk and he himself continued until 11 of the clock at night very disorderly and the next day following.

The last day of July the said Nation did much disorder himself at the house of one Richard Pole so as the man of the house could not be in quiet for him and his companions but was forced to send for the officers if not withstanding he continued in his drunkenness and encouraged his companions.

7th day of August last past the said Nation did very much disorder himself at the houses of Christopher Trowbridge and Thomas Bird all the night long.

19th day of August last past this Nation being arrested with a warrant of the peace and going to the justices he called Robert Taylor and said come ye forth Mr Wyndham's bailiff for I will run away and reported in scoffing manner towards Mr Wyndham that he sat as a Justice and when the officers dost bring in bills of presentment he would then take it in his hand and throw it back again and made a mocking of Mr Wyndham's worship.'

Even a person who should have known better caused offence. In a Presentment, dated 19th June 1694 to the Dean and Chapter of Wells by the Churchwardens, (a Presentment was a list of all things that had gone wrong), it listed that:

'The Church bounds to be out of repair.

(Music was provided by an orchestra since) *the double bass was to be repaired by Burge and Stallenge.*

Bounds to the Parsonage to be out of repair.

(Now the meat of the matter) - *The clergy.*

Item we do present, Mr John Musgrove, Curate, for not catechising of children, and for marrying of strangers the doors having been shut, and kept out the Clerk, and for the register being cut whilst it was in his custody and for being disorderly and scandalous and an unseeming minister in being drunken on Christmas Day and keeping company with lewd women.'

Turbulent Years - Sir John Stawell

In 1626 Sir John Stawell of Cothelstone bought, from John Wroth of Durrance in Middlesex, the Manor of Bishops Lydeard for the sum £4,500, an event that was to affect the lives of the inhabitants of Bishops Lydeard and Cothelstone for the rest of the century.

On 9th December 1617 Sir John Stawell, at the age of 18, married Elizabeth, daughter and heir of Sir Edward Hext of Ham, near Somerton, Somerset. Sir Edward was MP for Taunton and Sheriff of the County and had built for himself, at Ham, *"one of the best houses in the West of England"*, and also the Church, in which he was to be buried after his death in 1624. Elizabeth had previously been married to Sir Ralph Killigrew (died 1616) and through her second marriage to Sir John Stawell the Ham estates were to pass into his hands. John and Elizabeth had eleven children.

At the outbreak of the Civil War the Marquis of Hertford was sent by the King to the West Country to raise an army through *"gentlemen of the prime quality and interest in those parts, are likely to give as good examples in their persons, and be followed by as many men as any such a number of gentlemen in England could be"* - Sir John Stawell was one of these gentlemen. The Marquis issued warrants *"to draw together what volunteers could suddenly be gotten for services and bring to Wells what men, horses and arms they could muster"*. Sir John's two eldest sons went to their father's estates, John to Ham and Edward to Cothelstone and Bishops Lydeard. They returned three days later with 20 men, 40 horses and a wagon full of arms. The next day Sir John sent word to the Marquis that, *"Sir John Stawell's Regiment of trained bands was ready to marche"*. The Regiment comprised of a cavalry company, infantry company and a third company partly on horse and partly on foot called *Dragoons*.

By May 1643 Bishops Lydeard increasingly echoed to the sound of horses and wagons carrying arms to and from the Church tower, the Manor House at Cothelstone and Taunton Castle. Sir John was now in command of the town of Taunton that had surrendered to the Marquis. He had a garrison of 800 men but a year later Taunton was to fall to the Roundheads under the Earl of Essex. The circumstances were *"when Prince Rupert raised his siege from Lyme, he had unhappily drawn-out the garrison at Taunton under Sir John Stawell - a person of that eminent courage and fidelity that he would never have given it (Taunton) up - and left only 80 men in the castle to be kept by a lieutenant, who basely gave it up as soon as Essex in his passage demanded it, for which the lieutenant deservedly afterwards suffered death "*.

In July 1645 the Parliamentarians besieged Bridgwater. They attacked and entered the town on the 21st driving Sir John's regiment back to the bridge and over the river dividing the town. On the 22nd the Royalists refused to surrender their part of the town and Sir Thomas Fairfax offered safe passage for all the women and children - this included Lady Stawell and her children. On the same day Bridgwater was set on fire and the next day surrendered to the Parliamentarians. Sir John surrendered at Exeter and spent the next 14 years in Newgate Prison and the Tower of London. It was written of Sir John, *"that he was a great Chymist, he would say he learned patience himself by looking at the inconvenience of impatience and anger in others. And to keep his body in a temper suitable to his soul, for many years ate no breakfast, that his stomach might be cleansed, and its superfluous humours consumed before he came to dinner, saying that those who went with a crude stomach from one meal to another, without any extraordinary use of exsiccations as the ginger, oranges, lemons, horseradish roots etc would hardly escape the scurvy, if they did the dropsie".*

During his incarceration Sir John, apart from fighting for his own life, had to suffer much sadness. All his estates were sequestered, Edward was wounded and captured at the battle of Arlesford, Hampshire and all his estates, like his father's, were to be sold on account of his treason against Parliament. Edward went to France where he died having never really recovered from his wounds. Thomas, the fourth son also died in France. Ferdinand, Richard, William and Robert, the younger sons, died whilst he was imprisoned. His eldest son, John, became deranged, so Sir John made his third son, George, his sole heir and provided for his only remaining son, Ralph. Meanwhile Lady Stawell, who was living with her children at Cothelstone, having repaired the Manor to a habitable state, was constantly battling to get her £500 yearly settlement, granted by Parliament, from the Cothelstone estate. Henry Bovett, who was the trustee appointed by Parliament to administer the estate, together with the tenants, conspired to put as much of the monies into their own pockets. Elizabeth unfortunately died in 1657, so was never reunited with her husband.

A year later Robert Lawrence, bailiff, living at Bagborough, reported to his master, *"that Bovett had ordered the taking down that part of the north wing over the dining room of the derelict manor house as far as the second story, and had also had all the lead removed off the roof and melted it down using the joists and timbers available".*

Cothelstone Manor after the bombardment of the Civil War

Sir John was released in 1660 to witness the Restoration of the Monarchy and all his estates were restored to him. However the previous 14 years of trial and tribulation had taken their toll on him and he died at Ham on 21st February 1662, aged 62.

Bishops Lydeard was to witness the grandest funeral ever to pass through its streets.

There were over 200 in the funeral procession from Ham to Cothelstone - most on horseback. The procession had left Ham on Tuesday 22nd April and that evening arrived at Bishops Lydeard. His body, in a chariot covered with black velvet, was placed in St Mary's churchyard for the night, attended by his domestic servants. The following morning the procession of knights, gentlemen, officers and servants reassembled for Sir John's last journey to Cothelstone. The morning's silence was broken by the sound of two trumpets at the head of the procession followed by all his bailiffs, including William Nupper, junior, for Bishops Lydeard and Richard Dawe for Cothelstone. Two more trumpets headed the brightly uniformed Heralds at Arms: the gauntlet and spurs born by Francis Sandford, *Rouge Dragon*, the helmet and sword born by Robert Chaloner - *Blewmantle*, the coat-of-arms born by R. Dugdale - *Norroy King of Arms*. The silent onlookers remove their hats and bowed their heads as the chariot, pulled by six plumed horses, passed by the almshouses. Sir John was laid to rest beside his wife in the Church at Cothelstone.

The tomb of Sir John and Lady Elizabeth Stawell in the Church at Cothelstone

On Thursday 18th June 1685 many villagers made the five mile journey to

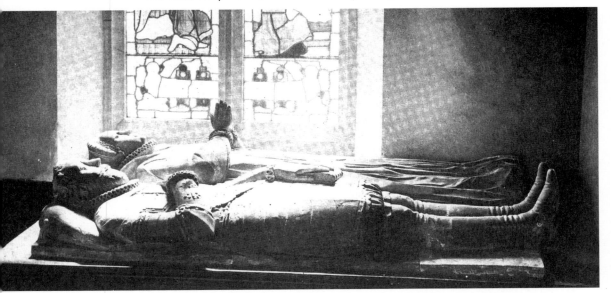

Taunton to line the streets to witness the entry of the Duke of Monmouth into the town. The streets were strewn with flowers, the houses and doors were adorned with green boughs, herbs and flowers and the windows were thronged with spectators. Bishops Lydeard would have received the news that on the Saturday morning the Duke had allowed himself to be declared King in Taunton's marketplace. Failure of the rebellion led to the infamous trials held by Judge Jeffries and part of this gruesome passage of English history was to be played out at Cothelstone.

Ralph, the only surviving son of Sir John Stawell, had been made Lord Stawell,

Baron of Somerton, in recognition of his father's services. He had also patched up the old manor house in 1681 to be used as a farmhouse. Although a supporter of the monarch, Lord Stawell was vehemently opposed to the cruelties of Jeffries. When summoned by Jeffries, he refused to see him. This resulted in Judge Jeffries sentencing Colonel Bovett to be hung from the arch at Cothelstone. Many villagers trooped up the lane behind the wagon carrying Bovett and a Mr. Blackmore, also sentenced to be hung, to watch the event.

Lord Stawell sold the Manor of Bishops Lydeard to John Periam, whose family had, for years, been wealthy wool merchants.

*The gateway arch at
Cothelstone Manor*

— Two —
Tales from the Eighteenth Century

Tales from the Eighteenth Century

The acquisition of the Manor of Bishops Lydeard by John Periam eventually brought about the formation of the large Sandhill Park estate. On his death in 1755 he bequeathed the estate to his grandson, John Lethbridge. The influence of the Squire would have been keenly felt in the village of Bishops Lydeard. Most were tenants of the Manor living in a tied cottage or farm. It is probably true that life in the village improved as the cottage homes were better built and maintained, being inspired by a paternalistic desire to see estate workers better housed and, as a result, more contented and loyal. It is said that Sir Thomas Lethbridge jumped from his horse and marked out on the ground with his riding crop saying, *"Build me a row of cottages here."* They became known as 'The New Buildings' - the row of cottages in Church Street opposite the Church.

Most youngsters born locally would go to work either in the house, grounds or on the farms. Service was practically the only work available for girls but a girl would gain valuable housekeeping skills. Most of life was lived out in the servants' hall under the watchful and exacting eyes of the butler, housekeeper and cook. Head servants ruled the house with regimental discipline in order to attain the high standards demanded. There were no labour-saving devices and servants worked long and hard to keep the house, with its bedrooms and richly furnished reception rooms, running like clockwork. Servants had strictly defined roles from the scullery maid, whose kitchen duties included laboriously polishing copper jelly moulds and pans with silver sand and vinegar, to the butler who was entrusted with the wine, silver and keeping proper conduct at meals. For many servants, however, the Lethbridges remained distant figures, but like all employers gossip and stories would have followed them.

Hill House c 1730 built by John Periam, later enlarged by John Lethbridge and renamed Sandhill Park.

The Lethbridge Legend

Samuel Izacke, Chamberlain of Exeter, wrote a curious tale in 1731 in his "Remarkable Antiquities of Exeter". According to him the first Lethbridges came to England before the Norman Conquest for the purpose of rape and plunder. Izacke tells the story: *"Ragnar Lodbrog (leather breeches), a nobleman of royal blood among the Danes, was flying his hawk near the sea shore when, together with its game, it fell into the sea. To save the bird Lodbrog took out his boat but the violence of the Tempest, which suddenly arose, drove him to a place called Roddam in Norfolk. From there he was brought to the King, Edmond, to whom he declared his birth and adventure, and for his skill in hawking, in which he excelled, the King entertained him kindly.*
Beric, the King's Falconer, was much troubled with envy at this, and spying his time to single out Lodbrog, murdered him in a wood. When a spaniel dog discovered the body, Beric was suspected of the crime, convicted, and sentenced to be put into Lodbrog's boat and committed to the mercy of the sea. Fate decreed that by a strange accident he was driven on to the shore of Denmark near to the place where Lodbrog had put to sea".

The boat was known to be Lodbrog's and the Danes rightly were very suspicious of its new owner and questioned him thoroughly. Beric, however, managed to lie his way out of this predicament and convinced them that Edmond, King of the East Angles, had murdered Lodbrog. The Danish King welcomed the excuse to raise an army, to which he gave command to Hunguar and Hubba the two sons of Ragnar Lodbrog.

Izacke takes up the story again: *"to encourage them to avenge their father and bring success to their enterprise their sisters wrought with their needles in an ensign the shape of a black Raven, a bird of ill-omen designed to strike dread into the hearts of the Anglo-Saxons. Hubba landed at Appledore in the days of Alfred the Saxon monarch, but the Danes were so valiantly withstood that they lost twelve hundred men, their banner taken and Hubba slain whom they buried on the shore near his ships."*

This landing and defeat of the Danes in 878 is written in the Anglo-Saxon Chronicle and to this day the people of Appledore point to Hubblestone Rock as the burial place of Hubba Lodbrog. (However it is far more likely the battle raged near Cannington and the River Parrett). Maybe Hunguar survived or some of the slaves were spared, and they took as a tribal rather than individual name, 'Leather Breeches'. It is not beyond the realms of imagination to see that three centuries later the name had become Lethebrooke and later still Lethbridge. By 1199 certainly an Ogier de Lethebrooke of Lethebrooke, Devon existed. However let us not dwell on the family history but look at some of the characters and events occurring after the Lethbridges came to Bishops Lydeard.

A Neighbourly Squabble

John Lethbridge, grandson of the first Thomas Lethbridge of Hill House, renamed the house Sandhill Park. He had made a good marriage to Dorothy, from the wealthy Buckler family, and so was able to enlarge the house and estate. It was at this point, around 1785, that the relationship between John Lethbridge and his neighbour, John Winter, had become so bad, that over the next thirty years they constantly took each other to court over whatever pretext they could find. Usually they accused each other of illegal fishing, diverting watercourses, poaching and obstructing property with illegally built walls and gates.

It became really ugly in 1812 when a case was heard at Taunton Assizes, in which John Lethbridge was accused of an assault on John Winter *"in pulling him down from a wall at Ash Priors mill pond"*. In retaliation a case was brought by John Lethbridge against John Winter *"for challenging him to a fight on the same occasion saying, I'll meet thee at any time and place and with any weapon thee shall think proper."* This all went on until 1814.

To rub salt into the wound John Lethbridge had received a baronetcy in 1804, "for services to the King in troublous times." However, had John Winter known of a certain indiscretion in 1799 he would have had a field day and John Lethbridge would not have become Sir John! The story can now be told.

A Dark Secret

Between 1799 and 1814 there were many letters written to Mr Beedon, a solicitor, concerning a Mary Jane Viall and her illegitimate child that was fathered on her by John Lethbridge. These letters include the way she was committed to Ilminster jail for debt on two occasions, and how she finally managed to attract the attention of a Mr Godwin from London and seduce him into marriage.

This is the first of the many letters from Sir John to his solicitor:

Dear Sir

It has been agreed that five shillings a week be allowed and paid for its maintenance and that it should be regularly paid into the hands of the officers for the time being and that the mother might have it from that, in order, if she choose to look after the child herself, but if she preferred giving up the child it will be properly put out to nurse and looked after by them. Mr Lethbridge will not hear of any other forms, as the above is amply sufficient for the protection, care and maintenance of it. Take care to avoid all degradation of the lady's character, which is too pure and immaculate to be touched upon by any human being.

She desires it that I would not send a man again as it is so highly disagreeable to her. I wish some means could be thought of to get this itinerant lady back to Brislington (near Bristol) where I believe she has gained a settlement of £20 per annum or to cause her to move out of this neighbourhood with bag and baggage. I remain, dear Sir, your humble servant, John Lethbridge.

Although none of the letters say whether the child was male or female, it is recorded that the house, called Fairwater, lived in by the Headmasters of Taunton School, was previously a lunatic asylum. Early in the 19th century it is written that one of the inmates had escaped and was wandering the town claiming she was the daughter of a Peer of the Realm. It is quite possible she was speaking the truth because in those days the asylum was the means of dealing with the unfortunate secrets that were not supposed to be let out!

The Ghost of Combe Wood

Returning to John Winter. The Winter's lived in Court House, Ash Priors. They owned a large portion of that parish and also land in Bishops Lydeard, Combe Florey, Halse and Lydeard St Lawrence. They had built a large tower in the keeper's Lodge in Combe Wood, from the top of which the keeper could keep his eye on the wood and obtain a glorious view of the surrounding country. It could have been built to annoy John Lethbridge by allowing persons to overlook his land!

Squire Winter, as has been shown, did not have a reputation for civility and high-mindedness. He was rather given to swearing at anyone with whom he came into contact and as a result many of his misdeeds or villainies were probably wished on him. Whatever his faults John Winter loved Combe Wood and he often took walks there, clad in brown velvet shooting coat and breeches. After patrolling the wood he would come and rest on the gate leading into the wood.

At last the old gentleman died, quite unrepentant, and no doubt the gatherers of wood, poachers and commoners, together with the surrounding parishes, breathed a collective sigh of relief! However they were not to be rid of Squire Winter that easily. His sins would not let him rest and after being buried he returned to his familiar haunts not only by night, as is the custom for a spectre, but also during the day. One Sunday afternoon two men saw him leaning on his favourite gateway but by the time they came up to him he had disappeared. Petitions were made to two or three clergymen to "read away" Squire Winter - that is to say prayers which would effectively banish him to the spirit world. In due course three Reverend gentleman *"came up to a certain ground near Bishops Lydeard and not only read him away but also helped to wall him in"*. Squire John Winter has not been seen again.

Lydeard House Gardens

A Lady Before Her Time

Two other large houses were built in Bishops Lydeard in the 18th century - in 1740 Lydeard House by John Coles and later Lynchfield House by Thomas Charter, both attornies.

John Coles' only surviving child, Frances, lived in Lydeard House from her birth in 1742 to her death in 1802, apart from the five years (1774 - 79) when she was married to Thomas Hamilton. They lived in Bath where he set up as an apothecary. Long before the Women's Rights Movement existed some women became, either through luck or personality, leading figures in their own local worlds. One of these was Frances Hamilton.

Frances was 32 at the time of her marriage, her father had died a few years earlier, and she had taken on the management of the family property. After her mother died, Frances returned to Bishops Lydeard on the death of her husband and became an active farmer who did not employ a manager.

From her own pen Frances Hamilton gives an interesting insight into the local people who touched her life in the latter part of the 18th century. Work went on extending Lydeard House during 1787 - 88 and Mrs Hamilton seems to have found the craftsmen, masons and carpenters almost uncontrollable. They came and went as they pleased: *"sometimes they came, looked and went away again, sometimes they came when I was out, I found it impossible to discover whether they had done any work or not."* She had employed William Hill, as carpenter and her most frequent complaints were directed at him: *"William Hill came here but what he did I could not be informed. Thomas* (her manservant) *is witness to this." "Bill Hill and the masons were drinking at the Bell and under the lime trees the whole day." "Winters* (employed by Hill) *worked two hours and then went to the Bell and drank the rest of the day." "John Hill* (William's son) *after doing a little work spent the remainder of the time talking to Tailer and taking and eating my nuts and apples."* It seems remarkable that the major extension works were finished by the end of 1788 considering the close proximity of the Bell! Strangely, William Hill continued to do odd jobs for Mrs Hamilton for years afterwards, still attracting the same kind of complaints.

Farming her land was her main business and Frances, even on her small farm, required the labour of a sizeable team of men - there was no mechanisation in the 18th century. Even horse-drawn ploughs had not made an appearance and oxen did her ploughing. She had two horses in 1796 - a mare called Pleasant and a horse called Bob and they were used for carting heavy loads such as stone or coal, or as a means of transportation for herself: *"God preserved me from death from a fall from my horse."*

Frances Hamilton was then in an anomalous and delicate position for a woman, she had to direct and organise the work of men. It is interesting to see how she coped with it. She paid her labourers a shilling a day and she refers to them as *"my people"* and she normally included at least one parish apprentice for whom she received a payment of one guinea annually from the Overseer of the Poor. She appears to have been an unusually benevolent employer. For instance, when there was no work one day for one of the workers, she gave him breakfast and dinner together with a present of fourpence. She writes frequently about one of her workers, a John Hooper. He seems to have been old, slow and inefficient but she paid him tenpence a day. Frances, however, grumbled about him frequently: *"John Hooper poor old man cannot do anything." "Hooper is capable of doing very little of any sort of work." "Hooper as usual doing nothing."* This went on for years but she never got rid of him. In the latter years of the century his pay went down to sixpence daily but it appears Frances made herself responsible for the whole of his rent: *"One year's rent for a house for John Hooper £1. 1. 6d."* He died in December 1801, six weeks before she did.

Birds keeping (Bird Scaring) by a Ploughboy

A farm worker could earn extra pay at haymaking and harvesting. Although it was common practice to pay harvest workers in liquor Frances preferred cash: *"Mowing the field before the house 2/6d. I gave them one shilling an acre instead of liquor."* Women were paid at half the rate of men and girls less than boys. This was not purely sex discrimination as women did not work the same hours or do the really heavy labour for example Bet Gard: *"Did weeding, picking stones or husbandry."* Children acted as bird scarers: *"Birds keeping by a girl 4/6d, by a ploughboy 6/9d."* Molecatching was another form of casual labour, paying 2/6d for an unspecified number of moles. Farm labourers worked all the daylight hours but went to bed when it was dark: *"Mr Charter came at 7 o'clock..... but the hour was late the people being gone to bed."* Making every possible allowance for changes in the value of money, it is clear that farmworkers wages were pitifully low.

Servants in the house were paid differently. They were hired by the year and also received food and clothing. A typical contract was drawn up by Mrs Hamilton in 1783: *"Abraham Cavell agrees to live with me one year, to give at the end of this year a month's warning or a month's wages, for six guineas and a suit of fustian* (coarse cotton fabric with a pile like velvet) *clothes, coat and waistcoat and a pair of buckskin breeches and a hat. If I choose to keep him one year he is entitled to carry with him the suit. But is not entitled to greatcoat or boots which he wears of mine."*

There were two men servants and four maids working in the house and occasional "dailies" who worked partly in the house and partly on the farm. She complained about the servants as she did about the labourers. Of a manservant she wrote: *"Went away from his work from 2 o'clock to 4 o'clock playing fives against the Church tower with the exciseman."* Of a maidservant: *"Betty Murch lived with me one year and three quarters and I believe she is honest and can be a very good servant but a more impertinent one was never in being."*

The Great Water Dispute

As a woman, Frances Hamilton was prevented from standing for Parliament or sitting on the local bench alongside the others landowners, like Lethbridge, Charter and Winter, but this did not prevent her doing battle with her neighbours when she thought her rights had been threatened.

There was a dispute over a watercourse, which flowed across Terhill Meadow from its springhead into the lane adjoining, down the side of the hedge of that meadow, into the ditch on the western side of Firlongs, through the coppice and into the little brook called Pixie. This water irrigated Frances' fields known as Fiveways and Washbrook. By early 1791 the water supply failed and Mrs Hamilton believed the stream had been diverted from its ancient course by Mr Slocombe, of Terhill House (see map p.32), and his tenant farmer John Bond. This was true. Mr. Slocombe, amongst his many freaks and fancies over landscaping, had diverted the water at Pilgrims to supply three ponds. The battle commenced by sending a letter to Mr Slocombe through her lawyer, Thomas Charter who lived across the fields in Lynchfield House. Mr Slocombe promised to remove the obstructions: *"Mr Slocombe said I may do as I please, beat down the boys."* (The 'boys' were obviously the objects that were diverting the water). So Frances went to see the obstructions for herself and Mr Charter collected evidence from the villagers as to the ancient water course. She was to lead her retainers on the field of action: *"John Hooper attended me to Pilgrim's Barn, where the water comes out of Bishops ground, and turned it into its ancient course. I met Mr Slocombe opposite the upper boy. Mr Slocombe accosted me saying he would do anything to oblige. I then told him I had been doing this, looking at the water which then ran down its course and asked him if he would own having turned it there, pointing to the Pilgrim's Barn. Upon which he said that he saw what I was at and so rode away home."*

Later things became more serious when the 'boys' were moved. *"Richard Lindon went up to Pilgrim's Barn to turn the water and John Bond would not suffer him to do it and by threats send him back to Washbrook. Richard Lindon and Thomas Vesey turned the water into its ancient course, and Joseph Hill, Mr Slocombe's workman, turned it into Mr Slocombe's new made pond and so they continued doing all of the day turning it forward and backward, and Mr John Bond also came and first turned it into the pond and cursed and damned Thomas Vesey and throwed mud upon Thomas Vesey and then went to Terhill and came again with Joseph Hill and then Mr Bond tried to take away Lindon's shovel. He afterwards snatched Thomas's shovel out of his hand and turned the water into the pond again and then left, Joseph Hill staid and he, Thomas and Richard Lyndon the rest of the day until toward 6 o'clock turned the water forward and backward."*

A neighbour now intervened: *"Mr Gibbs (tenant of Cothelstone Farm) said we were both wrong, myself and Mr Slocombe, for part of the water should run for pot water and the rest should go down the road towards Fiveways without a doubt, that Mr Bond was in the wrong to take it all his way and I was wrong to take it all mine for some must go down into the village for pot water."*

Mr Slocombe offered to lower the depth of his pond and Mr Charter informed Mrs Hamilton that she might not win if she took the dispute to court. She did in fact start legal action in March 1791 but unfortunately we do not know the actual outcome. Certainly Edward Jeffries, who had bought Terhill House by then, supported Slocombe and contributed towards the costs of the case. It is certain that a settlement was reached and it was not to Mrs Hamilton's liking: *"Pretended friends occasioned me much injury and abandoned me, some from interest..... The surprise and grief I felt, forced my eyes to overflow with tears."* On 23rd December 1791 she wrote: *"Signed that iniquitous covenant between Mr Bond and myself."*

Nothing more was heard about the great water dispute.

Spare a Thought for the Poor

It is amazing the amount of paperwork that the poor generated. It is easier to recreate the life of a pauper in Bishops Lydeard than it is, for example, a farmer. The average farmer's life story, in the documents created, have not withstood the test of time because they were not involved with officialdom. It is the poor that are the best-documented slice of society that we have.

Through the 18th century the Law of Settlement and Removal operated. The humbler people of society were expected to remain in their Parish of Settlement. If you wanted to move elsewhere you had to take with you a certificate signed usually by the Vicar, Churchwardens and Overseers of the Poor saying that if you fell on hard times and needed relief in terms of money from the Overseer, then your original Parish would bear responsibility. If the Overseer was not certain of your origin then you were questioned - you took an Examination. This was to show how and where your settlement might have been obtained. The rules stated that: if you were of legitimate birth you took the Parish of Settlement of your father. You could change this settlement by serving an apprenticeship in another Parish, by doing a job for a year and a day, renting a tenement worth £10 year or by serving parish offices such as a Churchwarden, Overseer, Tithingman etc.

These Examinations sum up the lives of the most lowly members of society, in the following case at least a whole generation can be reconstructed:

"The Examination of John Wescott now residing in Bishops Lydeard on 9th May 1800 touching the place of his last legal settlement. Ye have heard and he believes he was born in Bishops Lydeard (circa 1769) and when he was about seven or eight years old he was bound by the overseers and churchwardens of the said Parish, apprentice to a farmer Cordwhent of Bishops Lydeard. He served the said farmer under apprenticeship until he was about 19 years old, when he runned away from the said farmer Cordwhent and went to the Parish of Old Digbeth in the County of Warwickshire. He worked as a day-labourer for a Mr Dunn at the George Inn for about a month, then he went into the Parish of Dudley in the County of Worcester where he worked as a day-labourer for about three years. Then he went to the Parish of Tongue Norton in the County of Shropshire where he worked for about one month, then he went to the Parish of Lower Hefford in the County of Oxford where he worked as a day-labourer for about three months, then he went to the Parish of East Malling in the County of Kent as a day-labourer for ten or eleven months and he believes that his master, farmer Cordwhent never heard where he was from the time he left him until after his apprenticeship expired. About nine years ago he intermarried with Elizabeth Evington by whom he has four children, namely John aged seven, Elizabeth aged five, Joseph aged four and Mary aged about one year. About two months after he married he took a house in East Malling aforesaid of Sir John Twiston at the rent of £3 per year and that ever since he rented the said house he has paid Church rents and poor rates in respect of the same, but does not believe he was rated in his own name to the poor in respect of the said house but apprehends that the rate stood in his landlord's name. This examine says he hath done no other act than as above mentioned to gain a settlement to his knowledge. Signed with the mark of John Westcott."

By means of this examination Bishops Lydeard could show that the Parish had no responsibility for John Westcott, so they sent him back to East Malling.

The next example is of the examination of William Twigg: *"now residing in the Parish of West Bagborough touching this place of his last legal settlement, 1789, who said he was born in the Parish of Lydeard St Lawrence as he has heard and believes and when about 14 years old he bound himself apprentice to one John Biss of Tolland and served him until he was 21 years. He then hired himself to one Nicholas Labour of North Petherton with whom he lived as a yearly servant for seven years for the following wages viz: £4.15s for the first year and six guineas for every year thereafterwards. This dependent then worked with his father in Bishops Lydeard by the week for the space of about two years he then married Elizabeth, his present wife, and afterwards rented a public house and a field of ground in the said Parish of Bishops*

Lydeard for the amount of £6.10s a year. At the same time rented a lime kiln in the Parish of Cothelstone for the amount of £5. 10s a year, the whole amounting to £12 a year. He held this said tenement for the space of three years, residing the whole time in the said house in Bishops Lydeard and this dependent has worked as a labourer ever since he acquitted the said public house and has not done any other act to gain any other settlement. Signed with the mark of William Twigg."

By this examination West Bagborough were able to give Bishops Lydeard ratepayers the responsibility for supporting William Twigg.

The account books of the Overseers of the Poor for Bishops Lydeard, in the middle of the 18th Century, give a graphic insight into the lowest class of society in the village:

"Paid to Tamsin Brown 52 weeks at 18d per week, £3. 18s." (This is what it cost to support a pauper for a year).

"Abraham William's bill for coffins, nineteen shillings."

"Paid to William Morgan, tithingman, his bill for what he disbursed in the crowning of the men that were found dead in the lime kiln."

"Paid to Sarah Caswell in sickness twelve shillings, paid James Vosey in distress eight shillings.

"Carrying home of a family to Spaxton, with a Removal Order of Paupers, to the Parish where they belonged."

"Paid the watchmen for attending of the two fairs, four shillings."

"Paid to a travelling woman in distress three shillings."

Clothing and shoes for the poor, in the year, cost a small fortune. Mr Adams made clothes for £4. 15. 4d and Robert Hoare was paid for the making of shoes £1.13. 8d.

These are just a few items from one page out of several volumes, indicating the money that was paid, in Bishops Lydeard, for the care of the poor.

The system worked, it was a harsh system, but it meant that as far as every ratepayer was concerned they were doing their bit for the poor that belonged to them, but they did not feel that they had to support or maintain those who did not belong to them. There was a true sense of parochialism.

HIS Indenture, made
Year of the Reign of our S
Britain, France, and *Ireland,*
thousand seven Hundred and
Winter
Bishops Lydeard
Esquire and James
Parish, by and with the cor
Names are hereunto subscrib
aged eleven years a po
Francis's Meadow a

the Date of these Presents, until the said Apprentice shall ac
which shall first happen ————— acco
the said Apprentice h *or* said M *aster* faithfully shall
honestly, orderly, and obediently, in all things demean
Term. **And** the said *William Hadden* ——— for
with the said Church-Wardens and Overseers, and every of
every of their Successors, for the Time being, by these Pre

shall and will teach and instruct or caus

the Term aforesaid, find, provide, and allow, unto the said
Washing, and all other Things, necessary and fit for an Ap
be not any way a Charge to the said Parish, or Parishioners
Parishioners harmless and indemnified during the said Term
changeably have put their Hands and Seals, the Day and Y

Sealed and deliver'd in the Presence of *Philip Blewett*

A document drawn up in the reign of George the Third - 2nd April 1784.
It concerns Susannah Bodger, aged eleven, a poor child of the Parish of Bishops Lydeard, as witnessed by George Groom and John Winter, the Churchwardens and Charles Winter and James Allercott, the Overseers of the Poor. By this document she became apprenticed to William Hadden at the Mill, Bishops Lydeard, until she was twenty one or became married, whichever came first.
William Hadden's responsibilities were to teach and instruct or cause to be taught and instructed as an apprentice in Housewifery. He further had to provide Susanah with sufficient meat, drink, apparel, lodging, washing and all other things necessary and fit for an apprentice. Susannah was no longer to be a charge on the Parish.

Second — — Day of *April* — —in the *Twenty fourth*
ign Lord *George the third* — — by the Grace of God, of Great-
, Defender of the Faith, and fo forth ; and in the Year of our Lord One
ghty four — **Witneffeth** That *George Green and John* —
—————————————Church-Wardens of the Parifh of
e County of Somerfet —————————**And** *Charles Winter*
llorcott ————————Overfeers of the Poor of the faid
of his Majefty's Juftices of the Peace for the faid *County* ——whofe
ive put and placed, and by thefe Prefents do put and place *Susannah Bodger*
ild of the faid Parifh, Apprentice to *William Haddon in respect of*
his mills ————————with h*im* to dwell and ferve from the Day of
————————
lifh h*er* full Age of *Twenty one Years or day of Marriage*
to the Statute in that Cafe made and provided. **During** all which Term
in all lawful Bufinefs, according to h*er* Power, Wit, and Ability ; and
behave h*er* felf towards h*er* faid M*after* and all h*is* during the faid
elf, h*is* Executors, and Adminiftrators, doth Covenant and Grant, to and
, their, and every of their Executors and Adminiftrators, and their—
That the faid *William Haddon* the faid Apprentice in *Houswifery*
to taught and instructed —————— **And** fhall and will during all
ntice, meet, competent, and fufficient Meat, Drink, and Apparel, Lodging,
ice. **And** alfo fhall and will fo provide for the faid Apprentice, that fhe
e fame ; but of and from all Charge fhall and will fave the faid Parifh and
witnefs whereof, the Parties abovefaid to thefe prefent Indentures, inter-
ve-written.

WE whofe Names are fubfcribed, Juftices of the Peace for the
County —— aforefaid, (——————
——) do confent to the putting forth of the abovefaid
Susannah Bodger Apprentice, according to the intent
and Meaning of the above Indenture.

Jas Bernard

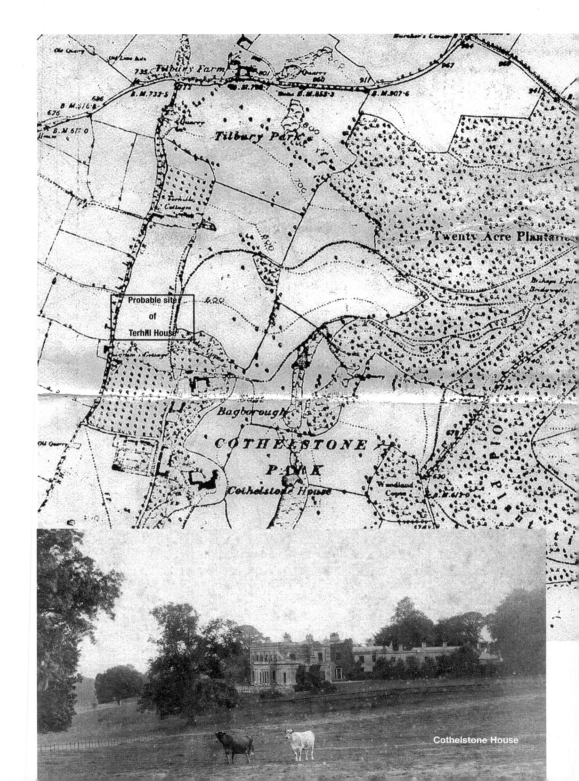

Probable site
of
TerhIl House

Cothelstone House

— Three —
Cothelstone

William Esdaile and 21 Lombard Street

A New House at Cothelstone

Employment

Edward Esdaile's Nature Notes

Cothelstone Farm

A Sporting Life

Cothelstone

Mr. Thomas Slocombe was an eccentric and he spent his time and monies on what he considered to be adornments to his estate but were in fact follies. It need only be mentioned that to reach Terhill House you had to cross two 3 ft wide shallow canals, divided by a strawberry bed, by means of a drawbridge. The house itself was an odd design having once been several cottages joined together and at each end two large rooms had been added. These formed the kitchen on the west end and the music room on the east. Although 120 ft long there were only two other rooms on the ground floor - a small breakfast room and a small drawing room. In the centre were two halls and an open colonnade. In 1792 Edward Jeffries purchased this house, as his country abode, and the Cothelstone Estate. He was a man of independent means having held the post of treasurer of St Thomas Hospital and had lived in a handsome house owned by the charity. His only child and daughter, Elizabeth, married William Esdaile.

Edward Jeffries who bought Terhill House and the Cothelstone Estate in 1792. The portrait was painted by Singleton in 1812

The Esdaile Family originated in France. In 1685 King Louis XIV revoked the Edict of Nantes. This had granted the Hugenots, who were Protestants, religious tolerance. So when the Edict was revoked many Hugenots fled from France to settle as refugees in England. One of them was Baron d'Estaile. All his property was confiscated and he lived in poverty and obscurity in the South East. The Baron's son became successful in commerce and anglicized the surname to Esdaile. He fathered James Esdaile.

William Esdaile and 21 Lombard Street

William Esdaile, was born on 6th February 1758, the 4th son of Sir James Esdaile, Knight of Great Gains in Essex and a wealthy citizen of London. After an education only fitted for the mercantile pursuits for which he was intended, he was placed as a clerk in the banking house of Messrs. Ladbroke and Co. It was here that he learned the skills which were to make him a first-class banker in the City of London. Sir James, who was made Lord Mayor of London, firmly upheld the aristocratic belief of first son's rights and made it clear to his numerous children that his large fortune would go to his heir, Peter - his son by his first marriage to Mary Jennings - and that his younger children would have to go out into the world and seek their fortunes. Peter, however, was a mild unambitious man who, far from desiring the entire wealth of his father, interceded on behalf of his brothers and sisters. Sir James' views softened and, despite retaining a decided partiality for his eldest son, finally was fair to all his children. On the death of Sir James in 1793 the world saw the unusual sight of his eight surviving children following the funeral in their respective carriages!

Louisa, daughter of Sir James' first marriage, had married a man called Hammet - better known later as Sir Benjamin Hammet. He was a Taunton man who gave his name to Hammet Street. The elegant tower of the church of St Mary Magdalene was almost hidden from view by buildings. The access to the

The Baron d'Estaile

Sir James Esdaile

1715 - 1793

Portrait by Sir Joshua Reynolds painted

when SirJames was

Lord Mayor of London in 1769

The Esdailes

William Esdaile

1758 -1837

Painted in 1835 by Leakie

Edward Jeffries Esdaile

1785 - 1867

Painted in 1821 by Barber of Derby

church was through a lane so narrow that it did not allow a carriage to pass without endangering pedestrians, and immediately opposite the entrance stood an old ruinous almshouse. Benjamin Hammet, having become MP for Taunton in 1784 and knighted in 1787, sponsored an Act of Parliament, in 1788, which allowed the creation of a spacious avenue to be built, not less than 36 feet wide, in direct line with the church from Fore Street. At his own expense he built the street - Hammet Street - of handsome houses, terminating in a large open space before the west front. This enabled a fine view of the tower to be seen from the Parade. Benjamin was an ambitious man with a mind far in advance of the times in which he lived, - 'a man of the world'. He began persuading his rich father-in-law of the immense advantages that would follow if Sir James were to form a new banking

Hammet Street in Taunton from an engraving by Coplestone Warre Bampfylde soon after the construction of the street.

house. It turned out to be an easy task and Benjamin masterminded the setting up of the bank. The first step was to acquire the old firm of Smith, Wright and Gray, bankers in Birchin Lane which he re-opened on 27th July 1780 as Sir James Esdaile and Co, with credit unlimited.

The quartet of partners was very strong. Sir James, Knight of the Realm and Lord Mayor, supplied the credit, Peter, his son, strengthened the chain. Thirdly, Sir Benjamin, enterprising, ambitious and in the prime of life, scoured the country, and to him was owed the establishment of its numerous banks through his wise judgment and understanding of his fellow men - selecting this man for his wealth and that for his sound understanding of banking. (1790 saw the formation of a Banking House in Taunton under the name of Hamett, Jeffries, Woodford and Buncombe, drawing funds on Esdaile & Co). In this way Sir Benjamin consolidated the Bank at Number 21 Lombard Street, a new house built by the firm. Last, but not least, came William Esdaile, the man of business. He could be seen perched on a high stool, absorbed in his task, hardly noticing those who came into the partners' office. He had neither the talent nor the inclination for general conversation, and although in the midst of active life, in fact, knew little or nothing of what was going on in the world out of banking hours and indeed took special care not to enquire.

Four years after the opening of the Bank he married the only daughter of Edward Jeffries and the three of them lived in the splendid house provided by St Thomas' Hospital. When in London, Sir Benjamin Hammet lived at 21 Lombard Street. It had no private entrance and all who visited or dined there had to walk through the offices where the 50 clerks could be seen at work. It was the custom to invite the numerous country customers to dinner and Benjamin was a most suitable host. He had the advantage of being a Member of Parliament and consequently of influence and authority. He was able to bestow many little favours and promise many big ones! The guests of the house never failed to leave the dinner table feeling gratified with their reception and conveyed this accordingly when they returned to their respective homes. It was found that the banking house soon became prominent in the City of London alongside the principal establishments of a similar nature.

William Esdaile, however, had little to do with the customers. Cautious and frugal himself, he was equally so with the money of his creditors. It was he who applied the brake when the other partners became flushed by the bank's success, pointing out to them their responsibilities and the dangers of making mistakes.

By 1800, 20 years after the opening of the banking house, Sir James Esdaile and Sir Benjamin Hammet had both died. Peter Esdaile was a sleeping partner only, without a talent for business, and living the life of a country gentleman at his residence in Great Gains. He received an annual allowance but was totally ignorant of anything going on at number 21. William Esdaile was then the true head of the firm and on him rested the responsibility for running the Bank. It was now that the traits of his character, hitherto concealed, were revealed. Fundamentally he lacked the moral courage to resist the slightest opposition and he found it impossible to judge men's characters. This manifested itself in his choice of partners and their unsuitability was in itself criminal and the ultimate downfall of the Bank must be dated from this time.

John Hammet, the eldest son of Sir Benjamin, had succeeded to a very considerable share of his father's fortune and also to his seat in the House of Commons. Even more valuable to him, however, was a partnership at number 21 Lombard Street. He was quite unfit to be a banker, not possessing any of the necessary qualifications for one. He had naturally elegant manners which had been polished by mixing in the highest society, devoted to extravagance, and he became known as the 'dashing banker'. His marriage to Miss Woodford, daughter of Sir Ralph Woodford, was very unsuitable since she encouraged and assisted him in every folly imaginable. It became absolutely necessary for the Bank to rid itself of such a dangerous encumbrance, and steps were actually taken to do so. However fate took a hand, his constitution sapped by excesses and deeply in debt, John Hammet died, hardly past the prime of life.

James Esdaile Hammet, a younger brother of Johns', had also been made a partner. He was in some respects much like his father, Sir Benjamin, a young man with a good brain, zealous and attentive in carrying out his official duties. However he possessed the other Hammet trait of the love of pleasure and dissipation. James was a remarkably handsome man with an iron constitution. As his mother's favourite, he was a spoilt child that continued into his adult life, making him an extremely bad tempered man who let no obstacle stand in the way of his desires. When at last he married, his character changed completely and he became very domesticated and an affectionate husband. However as a result of his excesses as a young man, his brain had been damaged a fact which, by 1823, had become evident to all. Up to this time and beyond, William Esdaile had been gradually imposing more of the running of the Bank on to James but this disastrous situation was not remedied until 1828 when James was finally retired from the Bank.

When John Hammet had died arrangements were made for Mr. Pascoe Grenfell to become a partner. Pascoe had been serving for some time as a clerk in the Bank and had been groomed to become a partner in it eventually. Although he came from a banking family, Pascoe was a complete failure. He was fully aware of the excessive advances of money being made by James Hammet, as James' mental instability increased, but unaccountably said nothing about it to William. Indeed Pascoe seemed to approve of and sanction many dealings.

When James retired, William had to look for another partner. Yet again William's inability to judge the character of men led to his disastrous choice of Rees Goring Thomas, his son-in-law, an attorney - as the saying goes 'of all men in the world an attorney makes the worst banker '. This was fully borne out for R.G. Thomas was completely unfit to have command of a large banking establishment in the City of London.

From 1828, on being taken on as a partner, he immediately exhibited a total lack of prudence in his financial management which led to such losses that the ruin of the Bank became inevitable. Even Pascoe Grenfell eventually became aware of this mismanagement since he said to his brother-in-law, another banker, that number 21 would not be tenable as a bank for much longer unless something was done. An inquiry was set up to look into the assets and liabilities of the Bank, the outcome of which was that, if a moneyed man could be found, the bank might be saved. After all it had been making upwards of £20,000 a year. At the eleventh hour an application was made to the Bank of England for a loan. £80,000 was made over to prop up the Bank and this was to be repaid by a certain date.

Meanwhile Thomas and Grenfell entered into discussions with several wealthy men about joining number 21, without involving William Esdaile. They were so concerned that their own portion of the profits would be minimised that they placed ridiculous demands on any would-be partner. So, when the date due for repayment of the loan to the Bank of England arrived, nothing had been accomplished. Number 21 found itself with insufficient funds to repay the loan.

On 16th January 1837 Sir James Esdaile and Co. ceased being a bank and stopped all payments. The Bank of England could not believe it, there was dismay and confusion in the City, people ran for gold at the Bank of England and general panic was about to follow. Payment was resumed again at number 21 within the day, as the Bank of England agreed to an advance of £500,000 providing all the property of the firm was made over to them, a further 28 banking firms advanced another £150,000 and loans from 70 country banks were taken up.

Number 21 was to wind up its accounts under inspectors from Glyn, Masterman and Unwin Sims and so this large and profitable banking house sank into oblivion in the hands of strangers. The two junior partners had friends to represent their interest whereas William Esdaile was not consulted. William would never hear a word said against partners, even from his eldest son, whom he sharply rebuked for his interference in such matters.

James Hammet had certainly got the better of William, for despite his revelling at night, the hours of business were spent assiduously at his desk. William could be bullied into anything and James's overbearing temper was enough to ensure that any profits came his way and not Williams'. As far as the other two were concerned, he just did not have the will or strength of character to prevent them taking the profits and ruining the Bank.

Despite the frequent losses he had to make good, William Esdaile got rich, being at one time worth about half a million pounds. This must be attributed to his small expenditure and his great tact and judgment in successful speculations on the stock market. There was much in his character to be respected and admired in avoiding a life of excesses. He was a very good host and, despite his often hasty temper and irritability, he never bore ill will, malice or uncharitable thoughts towards anybody.

William was an indulgent and most affectionate husband, very often to the detriment of his children, sacrificing their comfort and happiness to the whims and caprices of a sickly, selfish wife. While she lived everything took second place to her. When Mrs. Esdaile died in 1811 he transferred most of his affection to his daughters, although his two sons were regarded highly, William never disguised his preference for his daughters. He had a strong constitution, and was never ill, but felt for those that were, particularly in his own family, displaying a kind and sensitive manner. However he never made a friend in life, although one or two individuals were his companions in the latter part of his life, who certainly enlivened his days. One of these was his elder daughter who lived with him, in the house on Clapham Common, together with her husband, Dr. Richardson. Dr. Richardson was very valuable in being able to look after the old gentleman's health.

William Esdaile's main hobby, for many years, had been the collecting of fine works of art - pictures, drawings and prints. A vast number of these were brought to England at the outbreak of the French revolution in 1790 when the market became glutted with valuable and fine works. At this time William, finding money in his pocket, began to be seen at sales purchasing sparingly and cheaply. Doubtful of his own judgment and through a fear of being duped, he employed a highly respectable man called Thane to guard against it. The two were soon seen at all sales in London and the collection grew to 2300 drawings by 631 Masters and 4600 prints by 559 Masters. William also bought coins, china, books and minerals. This large collection became a solace to him in his leisure hours, away from the toils of Lombard Street. Towards the end of his life, when his mind was beginning to fail, he threw caution to the wind and commenced purchasing on a large scale at three or four thousand pounds a time. His collection at this time was almost second to none.

The life of William Esdaile was monotonous, broken periodically by visits to his father-in-law, Edward Jeffries, in Somerset. He passed many happy days at Terhill House leaving behind the cares of Lombard Street. On the death of Edward Jeffries in 1814 he continued his interest in the place, which had passed to his eldest son, Edward Jeffries Esdaile. It is difficult to believe that William, not having been mentioned in the will of Edward Jeffries, was anything but disappointed. However, Mr. Jefferies, had carved out his own fortune in London and was very proud of his success. He had a firm belief that the fall of the Bank was imminent and he knew the failings of his son-in-law, so it is certain that he did not wish to risk the careful earnings of a long life on the tottering foundation of the banking house - anyway William had a small fortune to his name.

In 1825 William Esdaile made his first trip to the Continent accompanied by Dr. Richardson and his wife, another daughter, Emma, and a Miss Wright. For nearly three months they toured Italy. He was so pleased with this tour that he started another tour in 1827 taking with him his elder son Edward Jeffries, and his wife, and one of their daughters, together with another son Henry. For three months they visited the romantic scenes of Switzerland. At this time William was a hail and hearty man of 70 years.

The following year, apart from a visit to Cothelstone and Dover, he stayed at Clapham and in 1829 he paid his final visit to Cothelstone, with Dr. Richardson and his wife. Although he apparently left his son on good terms, he never returned to Cothelstone saying that he was too old and his infirmities prevented him. However there had obviously been some family dissention since he embarked on an extended tour to Rome and Naples.

In 1832 William went to Dover - he liked watching the shipping in the Channel - but very soon developed a fever from which he recovered due to his robust constitution, (in others it would have been fatal). However his memory had gone which rendered him incapable of any business or of managing his property. His impaired memory and weakness of intellect meant he never read or wrote letters again. Each day he would look at his collection but began damaging some of his pictures, particularly his beautiful Claudes. They were put out of his reach and inferior drawings substituted. He never noticed, for by this time, as his elder son put it, "he was pleased with a feather and tickled with a straw".

Despite his weakened intellect, preparations were made in 1835 for a tour to Rome and Naples against the wishes of his elder son and others in the family. He went off in the autumn with Dr. Richardson and his wife, their young son, and a nursery governess, Miss Gann. They returned in May 1836 to Clapham to be greeted by Edward Jeffries Esdaile who noted that his father could not remember anything of the tour or the people he had met, despite being in remarkable health physically. In November of that year he had a heart attack whilst looking at his drawings and from that time he visibly declined in strength and spirit. He was nearly 80 years old.

The bank failed on 16th January 1837 and, just prior to his total confinement to bed, he had been called upon to sign the deed that conveyed away his whole fortune following the downfall of the Bank. He was looked after by his family during the next nine months and on 2nd October 1837 he breathed his last at his house on Clapham Common, aged 79. His remains were conveyed to a family vault in Bushill Fields where they were deposited by the side of his wife.

His elder son wrote, *"peace to be to his name and mercy to his soul. Providence in its wisdom cast a curtain over his eyes in his latter days and if he did perceive through it a picture of ruined fortunes, it was so kindly obscured and darkened that he acknowledged it not. He died indeed bereaved of worldly wealth but not of affection, of the remembrance or of the gratitude of one who subscribe himself - his eldest son"*.

A New House at Cothelstone

In 1791 Mr Edward Jeffries had purchased Terhill House for £10,963 together with the following farms, Cothelstone (£26,709), Dinhams (£6,650), Dean (£2,017), Toulton (£6,806), Waterpitts (£1,100), Broughton and Curry Moor (£7,033), Broomlands (£3,100) and Luxborough (£1,650). With other lands and tithes he paid a total of £70,735.

Terhill House was a wretched and uncomfortable house in a state of decay - it was said to be most unsuitable for a gentleman's residence. However Edward Jeffries,

Cothelstone House

**completed by Edward Jeffries Esdaile in
1820 and demolished in 1968.**

Staircase

Greenhouse which was destroyed by a gale in December 1929

Bridge across the road from the house to kitchen garden. The bridge still exists.

Kitchen Garden, with Orchard House built in 1864

Summerhouse similar in style to the 'Witch's House at Hestercombe

Drawing - room

being of advancing years and fully aware of his own ignorance of building matters, put off the building of a new house. He was also a perfect stranger to rural matters having lived the greater part of his life in London.

During the 22 years he lived in Terhill House his accounts showed that he did not make more than £800 from the timber on the estate - this would indicate that not much timber was felled during those years. In fact the opposite was the case as large and valuable number of fine trees, particularly elms were disposed of and the proceeds did not find their way into Mr Jeffries' pocket! Allegedly, according to his grandson, five individuals robbed him of thousands of pounds with the consent of the bailiff. The bailiff, when he left Mr Jeffries service, was worth £1000 with a young wife and several children to support. However he died in penury. One of the five later appeared in the Bankcruptcy Court where it was shown that he had made a profit from the timber of £1000.

When Edward Jeffries Esdaile became a permanent resident at Terhill House he put a stop to these nefarious activities. At that time the woods in Grove Coppice had just been condemned and work had started on the felling of some fine oaks. A timber merchant from Bridgwater requested a large oak tree to be sold to him. Edward reckoned the tree to be about 3 tons and asked £36 for it - which he got. This shows how valuable timber was to an estate. On recounting this to his grandfather and telling him that £36 were the proceeds of just one tree, Edward Jeffries did not believe his grandson even to his death in 1814.

Succeeding to the greater part of his grandfather's estate, including the stocks and shares of £66,652 - the annual income from which was £2760, and supported with money from his father, William Esdaile, Edward Esdaile set about the building of Cothelstone House.

The site had been chosen some years before and in 1813, Veitch, a planter from Exeter, was called in to lay out and plant a shrubbery adjoining the site. This was a wise move for during the five years of the house being built the trees grew and provided shelter and cover for the house. A plantation to the western front came about by chance. The bailiff of the time, making some holes with his stick, deposited acorns in them. These did well, being protected by firs, and with judicial thinning, the oaks gave good protection to the house by 1860.

The first stone was laid on 3rd April 1817, the stone coming from the quarry near Millbrooks Farm. The house, stables, outbuildings, kitchen garden and furniture (mostly from Gibbs & Co. in London) cost nearly £20,000 - £16,000 came from William Esdaile and the rest from Edward himself.

Cothelstone House was substantially built, designed by Mr Harcourt of Bath, who, being an old man at the time and living mainly in London, left the architectural supervision to Mr Manners also of Bath. On site there was a clever and first rate Clerk of Works by the name of Watson.

Edward Jeffries Esdaile moved into the new house in October 1820. Terhill House was then demolished.

Employment

A big house and estate in the 19th century employed a large staff to carry out the many types of work required to make it run smoothly and profitably. Cothelstone was no exception and Edward Esdaile in his journal gives accounts of those who lived and worked on the estate during the late Georgian and early Victorian era.

In 1832 he was paying tax on six men, one bailiff, two four wheeled carriages, four horses, one greyhound, four farm horses, one pony, five dogs and armorial bearings. The wages and conditions for a man at that time were: the butler £45 with no clothes provided, the footmen £16 with clothes provided, the coach man, William Hook, £32 with no clothes (he was also paid £5 to drive Edward when staying in London), the groom £12 with livery, Robert Reid, the gardener, was paid £60 with no clothes provided but he was given a cottage rent free, the bailiff was paid £41.12s with a cottage provided but no clothes, and finally the gamekeeper was given a cottage rent free but without clothes for the annual sum of £26.

John Cox was bailiff and for many years Joseph Fox had been the gamekeeper. Henry Gurnett took over as gamekeeper in December 1834 and remained in the post until he died suddenly on 20th December 1857. He had been in service at Cothelstone for 27 years but his health had been failing for the last two or three years of his life. He was only 47. The new gamekeeper, appointed on 11th January 1858, was Thomas Peak. On leaving the service of Mr. Lopes of Tetton House his conditions were agreed as £52 per annum, a cottage rent free, firewood and an issue of clothes yearly, namely a jacket, a waistcoat, breeches and leggings.

John Cox had become bailiff on 1st March 1828 and finally left this important job in 1841. William Morton, who would become the gardener in 1838, took it upon himself to do both jobs for an increase in wages of £10 to £70 per annum. By 1846 Edward Esdaile had given him notice to quit.

Not all jobs were filled by trustworthy men. In 1837 Samuel Treby was appointed footman in Cothelstone House. However soon after, he was transported for breaking and entering Mr. Tudeway's house in Wells where he had worked as footman.

There were others whom Edward mentioned for their long service and out of affection. William Hook left his service as coachman in September 1847 after 17 years and four months. William Rossiter had come into the service of Edward's maternal grandfather in 1799 as a footman and from long service in the family, William had become very much attached to them. On 6th April 1854, Edward Esdaile's birthday, William Rossiter died, and coincidentally in the same bed where Edward had been born. He left £1,200 to his wife, which on her death would pass to Edward. Four years later she died at the age of 81.

On 20th May 1864 James Gunston, the butler, left Cothelstone with his wife who was maid to Edward's wife for 32 years. Gunston had been with the family for 30 years.

The journal records one other interesting character relating to Blacky Tops Hole.

Around 1770 a cave existed in the lias rock within a small cover on Cothelstone Hill. At that time an eccentric man took up residence in the cave dividing it into two apartments by a door. He never slept in a bed but lay on some straw on the ground. He lived the life of a virtual hermit and the cover was left alone, only being known by the lime burners. It was a wild, out of the way place. Occasionally the man worked for local farmers but he was very reserved and had very 'unsociable' habits. His name was Black or Blackmore, hence the name given to the place. By 1863 the cave had subsided and debris had almost filled the entrance, although a stain of smoke could still be seen on the rock.

Edward Esdaile's Nature Notes

The seasons, weather and the wildlife played a major part in the lives of all the people on the Cothelstone Estate. Some of the pursuits would nowadays be forbidden. Here are some examples from Edward Esdaile's Journal in his own words.

In the winter of 1829-1830, which was remarkable for numerous flocks of wild fowl, particularly geese, there were those known by the name of laughing geese and numbers of which were killed. Whistling swans were often seen about and three alighted on the lawn of the Reverend Cecil Smith at Lydeard House, Bishops Lydeard. Within a few feet of the House two were shot at with snipe shot, only one, a young one, fell, but the other, badly wounded, flew to Taunton along the Vale and was finally killed, it proved to be a male and is now in the Taunton Scientific Institution.

In the year 1824 an Osprey Sea Eagle, a female, was shot on the pond at Sandhill Park. It was brought to me and I sent it to London to be stuffed by Leadbetter. I afterwards presented it to the Taunton Institution.

The year of 1814 was one in which the winter was a very severe. Much deer, game and small birds were starved in various parts of England. A deep fall of snow fell on 5th January and in the following April still remained under the hedges.

I find the most effectual mode of protecting young trees from the bite of hares and rabbits is to paint them with the stuff from the gasworks. It remains three years of service and no way injures.

In 1811 the rabbits began to get so numerous that it became a matter of necessity to reduce their numbers. Large parties were constantly shooting and ferrets and other means resorted to, but it was not until the use of wires were known and much attested to, that any material dimunition of the numbers was felt. Note - wires should be cautiously applied and only at those seasons of the year when hares are full-grown otherwise they will be caught in them. By 1859 gins or traps were being used successfully.

In the spring of 1834 an accident occurred at the lime kiln on Cothelstone Hill with the loss of three lives. The coroner's jury brought in their verdict "suffocated by the gas escaping from the kiln". The kiln was built in the spring of 1832.

1840. Sold at the Gore Inn, Bishops Lydeard, sundry lots of oak, elm and ash trees standing on several farms. The price of the whole was £1,224. All to be felled by July and taken away by Christmas.

14th September 1840 after an unexampled continuance of dry weather the temperature suffered a considerable diminution and rain at last seemed at hand. It commenced towards night in heavy storms. From the 13th April to this day there were but four hours of rain and this happened on 17th August, a period of five months and one day. The consequences of such a drought were apparent enough, the leaves of many trees falling off and the watercourses in very many places dry and in all reduced below their lowest average. The rain on the 17th August was heavy and saved the turnip crop going furrow deep but the meadows got little or nothing by it. It appears this extraordinary absence of rain was confined to the Western parts of England even not further eastwards than Wells enough fell at intervals to cause an abundant vegetation and on the Mendips might be seen a second crop, whilst on the rich lands around Bridgwater not a blade of grass was visible nor had been during the summer. It is needless to say that harvest time was the shortest known. Game of all descriptions bred well particularly partridges and hares.

In 1840 an instance occurred which showed the properties of the common snake. It was at the end of May after a day's Rook shooting that something was observed moving in the high grass and nettles beneath the trees. One person going to see what it was saw a snake having hold of a full grown young Rook by the wing. The bird was using endeavours to escape. The reptile in the meantime pulling him along through briar and brake. On an instinct that something was going on, I went to the spot and witnessed the fact as stated making however my approach without due caution the snake let go the bird and glided into the grass. After a minute or two he again appeared and once more seized his prey. The struggles of the two were brought so close to the spot where we were standing that the snake became alarmed and withdrew himself entirely. The Rook had a wing injured by shot, in other respects appeared well. The above fact proves how destructive the snake must be to game if he can swallow a bird the size of a Rook. What chance has a young pheasant or partridge?
A short time since a common snake was knocked on the head and left for dead. A

person coming by seeing the stomach of the reptile much distended, with his knife cut it open and took out a toad apparently just swallowed. He then wishing to preserve the skin of the snake for stuffing placed it on one side for security meaning to take it away. An hour or rather more might have passed before he returned to the spot, but when he did, nothing of the snake could be seen. One month afterwards a snake was seen swimming in a pond close to the place where the former reptile was left for dead with his belly cut open. The snake was caught and to the surprise of its captors proved to be the very same, the wound was healing very slowly and still was open.

<u>*Methods made use of to destroy pheasants and to guard against poaching at Cothelstone.*</u>

July and August

Generally in the last few fields of standing barley and oats the birds are about half grown and are caught by a long silk purse net lightly weighted being drawn over the corn at night by two men. The pheasants are sold to stock other manors and it is much suspected that the keepers of those manors will buy them especially when the birds are scarce with them.

To guard against poaching - no other way than by a night watch - farmers not liking to have their corn run over with dogs. This method would be employed to unroost the birds every evening until the corn is cut.

September and October

Some pheasants are shot when partridge shooting. Also towards the end of the latter month by means of nets heavily weighted down over the turnip fields. A vast number of young birds are thus destroyed.

Various means have been tried to guard and protect the turnip fields. Thorn bushes, stakes with knives therein, but no way is so good and safe as every evening to drive the birds from the roost.

November and December

Pheasants now begin to seek the covers some still roosting in turnips however. Many birds will be found at night on the trees and low bushes and night shooting has begun long before the leaves are off the trees - a long pole with a knife blade fixed at the end is sometimes made use of, but, the birds having been so wounded, it is supposed they fly some distance before they drop and maybe lost in the dark or fall into poachers hands.

The weather in which the poacher is found out at night is wild and windy and in the most violent storms of thunder and lightning. Nights of this sort must be particularly looked to - a gun can hardly be heard a few yards off and it is never too dark - something as many as 12 or 14 poachers have been seen together, some to find out the birds or their roosts and others to shoot so as to lose no time. Then again one poacher only will, at the commencement of night creep into a preserve, observe a bird or two, mark well the tree and towards morning perhaps enter and shoot once or twice, seldom however more than twice, the man not being in the cover more than 10 minutes. When a preserve is so visited, unless put a stop to, every bird goes with certainty. Feeding, to get the birds at home, should commence with November at the very latest and the best plan is to put the food in troughs. Birds are caught near them by gins and wires, also near the corn ricks in the fields, or in the runs through the hedges.

The winter of 1845 - 6 was the mildest almost ever experienced. Without frost or snow. About the middle of April there were three nights so cold and unseasonable as to be one of the means of the failure of the garden and orchard fruit. Of apples, pears, plums, apricots, peaches and nectarines there are none sufficient. Rains fell in good time to insure the grasslands being productive and hot weather setting in the last week of May forced vegetation exceedingly. So high was the temperature (between 75 and 80) that by the 20th June the garden vegetables, with the strawberries, were out of season. No rain has fallen during the month.

Winter 1850. During the whole of the winter, leave was given to various parties to catch rabbits on Cothelstone Hill, also on Toulton, Cushuish and Tilbury farms. The keeper and his four men constantly at work nearer home. No accurate account could reach me of the numbers killed - Babb the tenant of Toulton has killed 722. Edwards at Cushuish 600, my own men may be reckoned at bringing in about 240 per week for the last 16 weeks - 3800. At a guess therefore say 6,000 in round figures as a total to the end of January.

It is a matter of regret that artificial bodies of water should have their surfaces too often found infested by weeds. This was seen to a great extent on the large pond here that it was almost impossible to get a boat through. A pair of swans had young ones in the spring of 1853, six in number, and in the spring following not a weed remained on the water and, for the first time since the formation of the lake, the whole surface was clear of it. The swans had affected what numbers of men could not have done, but to their own detriment for they were deprived of food and to keep them alive they were daily supplied with barley. It is considered that three to four swans may be supported by the water allowing for some portions of weeds.

The number of rabbits killed by trapping and otherwise was some 11,000 during 1859, they were found in plenty again on commencing in 1860, catching in one night, 120 traps secured 160 rabbits.

27th August 1860. Wheat harvest commenced on Cothelstone Farm by means, for the first time, of a reaping machine, which appeared to execute its work well and rapidly, but not with profit.

On 5th August 1863 a limb of the great walnut tree standing in the field at Cothelstone called the Dodhay fell with a great crash. I was near it at the time and fortunately no cattle, of which many were in the field, suffered injury. The limb about five feet round was only supported by some two or three inches of sound wood, the remaining parts being quite hollow. To my great regret this aged and magnificent walnut tree, said to be the largest known, appears rapidly to be going into a state of decay. I have been told that during the Great War with France my grandfather was offered £300 for it by the English government in order to convert into gun stocks.

December 1864. In consequence of the abundant crop of apples, casks were not easily obtained to hold the Cider. Fine fruit could be had for about one shilling to one and sixpence per bag and in some instances were given away if asked for. As a matter of course the produce of the two orchards I keep was made into Cider, a tedious long job, but if kept intact for a level month probably will fetch a good price. As it is well known orchards under slovenly and careless management of the generality of farmers, never bear a crop two years in succession.

Cothelstone Farm

Since the devastation of the Stawell Manor House by Cromwell's cannons during the civil war, it underwent repairs sufficient for it to be used as a farmhouse in 1681. A series of tenants ran the farm for the next 160 years or so. When Robert Gibbs gave notice of his intention to quit the farm in 1853, after 40 years as the tenant (his father before him had been tenant for 32 years), Edward Esdaile decided that the time was right to update the farm and in particular restore the farmhouse to its appearance as it had been in the time of the Stawells.

Work started in March 1851 on clearing the site for the building of a new barn and linhay in the timber yard. Mr Pollard, a builder from Taunton, commenced building in the following month. The floors of new pigsties were laid from coal ashes and tar. From January to May of 1852 men began to deepen and prepare the ponds either side of the turnpike road as a reservoir for the water mill which was to drive the mill machinery. This machinery was purchased from Messrs. Stoddart, Raine and Pitts in Bath, for £240.

In October a large sale of stock was held on the farm. It was a big occasion with six to seven hundred people attending and a large dinner took place in the New Barn in the Barton yard. The livestock fetched high prices for the times - one lot of sheep reaching £3.10 shillings per head - altogether 828 animals were sold.

By 5th February 1853 two men finally completed the excavations to receive the water wheel and had built the tunnel through solid rock to carry the water to the wheel. A week later the wheel and machinery arrived from Bath together with a man to put it up. The reservoir took 98 hours to fill, as the springs were very low. The two plugs were then drawn to test the one-foot diameter earthenware pipes that had been laid from the reservoir to the mill house. As suspected they did not

NB.

A very cheap, and efficient manner of building small outhouses, and Linhays,

Erect posts the required space, use Slabs from the Sawyers pit, at the back taking the precaution of covering the Joins, place pieces of Timbers (Poles &) across and roof in with wallett with Thatch attop, - a good sized Shed can be got by this mode, for five pounds and which will last many years

It will be observed part of the Roof, hardly a Nail save to fasten rest upon a or what would   *no timber is used in any or sawn wood elsewhere in the construction the Slabs, which should sleeper of sound Oak, be better two feet wall*

stand up to the pressure and iron pipes had to be put in. A new wall was built in August in front of the New Barn to divide the Barton. This was done to make an enclosed space for the erection of a sawmill which was then attached to the water wheel. A year later the pipes that had been laid from the great pond were completed and water flowed to the wheel.

The use of water to drive machinery had already, in many parts of the country, been superceded by steam. So by June 1856 Edward Esdaile was driving his small sawmill by steam - it could cut 3816 feet of timber in $1^1/_4$ days. He decided to get a permanent steam engine and demolish the water wheel. On the 16th July 1857, an engineer and a man from Taunton began to take the large iron wheel to pieces. It took them two days - the wheel had only been in position for five years. A year later the foundation was laid and masons erected the scaffolding for the building of the chimney for Cothelstone's steam engine. They used secondhand Ham Hill stone costing £25 to build their hollow pillar. The engine, purchased from Mr. Parsons of Martock for £240, arrived in November 1858. Cothelstone had joined the steam age!

Back in July 1855 Mr. Wainwright came from London, as Clerk of Works, to superintend the repairs to the old Manor and also the erection of new cattle sheds. The sheds took 5 months to build and received their first ten bullocks in January

The structure of a Linhay described by Edward Esdaile in his journal

1857. The last main change to the farm decided on by Edward was to remove the barn and granary, erected in 1851, and rebuild them in the Great Barton. He also removed the high walls to open up the view of the restored Manor House.

Two men had started clearing the ruined wing of the old house in July 1855. Discussions had taken place between the tenants, Messrs. Stuckey and Steed, and Edward. The tenants wanted the work to be done on a larger scale than Edward thought was justified, so it was agreed that the tenants would provide £500 in cash and Edward would advance £200 plus the cost of materials. The architect, Mr Clarke from London, thought that the £700 would be sufficient to pay the workforce. The renovation was to cost in total £2000.

On clearing the wing the men made an exciting discovery. The Stawell dungeon was brought to light for the first time in 200 years since it had been buried by the cannons. Fetters and iron chains were found and the dungeon must have been a dark and damp place with only one very small window and small stream of water constantly running through the middle. In the wall above the dungeon they uncovered a strongroom which was some eight feet above floor level and, with iron doors, would have been very secure. The restoration of the Manor House was completed in 1856.

The ancient Porter's Lodge in front of the House was renovated, as for many years ivy had been forcing its way through the walls. The lead from the roof was recast and used again. Lastly the arch, which had spanned the road from Bishops Lydeard to Bridgwater, was removed and rebuilt, facing the House, and two smaller arches

Sketch of the treasury and dungeon drawn by Edward Esdaile

Interior of Treasury

Interior of Dungeon

added. So Cothelstone Manor was completed with its Barton, much as it appears today, enabling us to imagine how the Manor looked before the Civil War.

A Sporting Life

Shooting was not just a pastime but also an important means of getting rid of vermin. For example in the four years 1833-6 the following vermin were exterminated : polecats 29, stoats 58, voles 33, cats 35, hawks 41, magpies 82, jays 71, kites 3, squirrels 123, owls 33, daws 41, a total of 605. Rabbits were also shot as well pheasants, woodcocks, snipe and wood pigeons to provide food. During the Victorian era it became very fashionable to stuff the creatures that had been shot and exhibit them in the house.

Hunting started at Cothelstone when the Devon and Somerset Staghounds met for the first time there, in September 1840, to rouse a stag on the Quantocks. A six-year-old deer was found at Bagborough plantation close to the house of Francis Popham. After a chase of less than two hours the deer took to the sea at Watchet but was brought safely to land. Two days afterwards the animal was restored to his old haunts on the hill nothing the worse for wear.

A typically eventful meeting took place at the beginning of the month of October 1843, when the Staghounds hunted the Quantocks twice during the week, the hounds staying in the kennels at Cothelstone House. On the first day a stag was harboured in Cockercombe and roused by the tufters in about half an hour. The lay-on took place by Bagborough plantation and the pack carried on the running over Cothelstone Hill down Buncombe Bottom. The deer broke away for Broomfield towards Willyby's Farm. Here the chase ended, the stag having been shot by Mr. Henry Cogan, who was obviously waiting with that intention in mind. This was a most promising day's sport unexpectedly terminated.

Two days later, the hounds were out again. A stag was harboured close by Quantock Farm about half a mile from the place where the one before was found. From the time the deer jumped up, to the time the pack were laid on took a quarter of an hour at the most. Shortly after, however, another young male deer sprang up out of some furze on the hill in full view of the hounds. This deer was ignored by the hounds and they continued on their original quarry. Crossing the great woods over Cothelstone on up to Broomfield and from thence to Halswell Park. Here the field was well placed, because of the very hard, dry fallows and dusty roads, the pace was not so fast as to prevent the riders being close enough to the pack. The line continued through the Vale of Bridgwater by North Petherton until the Great Western Railway was reached. The deer was frightened several times by the many workmen on the line and plunged into one of the locks of the Taunton Canal to conceal itself. However the boatmen found it and adroitly flung a long rope over its horns. A quarter of an hour later the field arrived. Good care was taken not to injure the animal and it was carried to Mr. Bond's place close by and the following morning brought safely to Cothelstone and restored to the hills. The deer was a long-legged fine three-year-old not the least tired by the chase that had lasted two and a half hours. There was little doubt it could have run 10 miles further had not the railway intervened and frightened it. Hunting was to continue on the estate for well over the next hundred years.

By 1840 hare coursing had become established in front of the House during the months of November, December and January. Fourteen years later it had become an extremely popular and public event with some six to seven hundred people attending the meeting. The 1854 meeting was held opposite Cothelstone Farm for the first time as many hedges had been levelled and the grass was good. A silver cup (to be known as the Cothelstone Cup) was competed for by sixteen greyhounds and the Gore Inn Stakes was run for eight greyhounds. Many hares were found and thirty courses were run over four hours.

The meeting advertised for 27th and 28th January 1859 took place with ideal weather. The first day's coursing took place over ground in front of the House, however some 2000 people had turned up and greatly impeded the coursing. It was therefore decided that, partly to meet the now considerable expenses of the meeting and partly to limit the numbers attending on the following day, to charge one shilling for a ticket. The receipts from ticket sales were £36 so the crowd of 720 was much more manageable for the second day of coursing over Cothelstone Meadows.

The meeting had commenced with the two principle Stakes, firstly the West

The Hunt outside Cothelstone House 1929

Somerset Stakes for fourteen puppies, which was won by Mr. Miller's Merchant beating Mr. Bryant's Niagra, followed by the Cothelstone Cup for sixteen greyhounds of all ages, won by Mr. Bowle's Sarah. It cost the owners of the dogs the princely sum of £3. 10s to enter them, but the prize money was £20 for first, £10 for second and £6 each for third and fourth. Other stakes at the meeting were the Bishops Lydeard Stakes, Consolation Stakes and some other smaller events. An unusual incident occurred later when guests went to the dining room in the House - a hen pheasant had flown through a large plate glass window and was found dead on the carpet. The cost of replacing the glass was £8!

Another public meeting in December 1865 did not go according to plan. Some eight to nine hundred people had gathered at Cothelstone Arch but dense fog prevailed for the whole day over the valley and the meeting could not take place. In consequence of the great disappointment felt by so many it was decided to advertise another event in January and the Stakes were quickly filled and a big crowd again expected. On the Saturday evening at nearly ten o'clock, Mr. Stuckey of Cothelstone Farm and Mr. Hurst of Kingston requested to see Mr. Esdaile, saying they were representing local farmers. They pleaded with him to cancel the Coursing Meeting on account of the cattle plaque (presumably foot and mouth). Mr. Esdaile had no alternative but to comply in view of the numbers of dogs and people who would be assembled on the Cothelstone Meadows the following Wednesday, and he had just three days to give notification of the cancellation of the event.

A painting c.1840 by Miss Sweeting. It looks across the old road (in front of Dunkirk Memorial House) across Phiffin (original spelling) Meadow to the Church. The house on the far right was the Vicarage at the end of Piffin Lane - the site now occupied by the house called Piffins.

The Old Forge and Piffin Lane 1842.

— Four —
The Victorian Years

Family Fortunes

Winters at Watts

The Parochial School

A Diary of Village Entertainment -
Victorian Style

Have I got News for You

Edwardian Bishops Lydeard

The Victorian Years

As the 19th century progressed so the prosperity of Bishops Lydeard improved. The patronage of the Lethbridge family at Sandhill, the Esdailes at Cothelstone, the Winters at Watts and the Smiths, followed by George Sanders at Lydeard House contributed to the employment, support and well-being of the villagers.

The building of the railway was another greatly contributing factor. On 7th April 1859 a large number of people assembled in an enclosure at Crowcombe Heathfield to witness Sir P.P.F.P. Acland cutting the first sod of the Taunton and Watchet Railway. It was to open for general traffic on 30th March 1862. The railway rapidly became much used. Tradesmen found it more convenient when coming to Bishops Lydeard and Cothelstone, for orders and parcels arrived more quickly. The most notable improvement for the Cothelstone Estate, however, was the saving of labour in the haulage of materials. Lime from Donniford, coal from the harbour at Watchet, and Ham Hill stone could all be off-loaded at Bishops Lydeard station.

An agreement was entered into with a man to bring up small things from the station and take down the baskets of rabbits from Cothelstone for the onward journey to Birmingham. The man was paid sixpence a trip. The number of rabbits trapped in one night and sent down the next day could be as many as 125. The sale of rabbits to Birmingham became a lucrative business with over 6000 being trapped in a year bringing an income of over £200. By the early 1860's Charles Goodland and Son had built a yard at the station for coal, lime and bricks.

The village became virtually self-supporting. Nearly every trade which had to do with the commercial, industrial or personal wants of the inhabitants had its practitioner - saddler, butcher, baker, grocer, draper and plumber.

Dr Harry Roberts, who grew up in Lydeard Cottage (now called The Mount) as a young boy in the 1870's recalled:

I can see Mr Parry, our long bearded stationmaster, with his frock coat and a fresh geranium in his buttonhole each morning. I see Mr Trickey, the saddler, whose shop was just opposite Mr Lickfold, the butcher - the latter establishment more like a private house with a large and palatial larder full of great joints of meat than anything we think of nowadays as a butcher's shop. There was the carpenter, Mr James Saunders, with his sons Dick and Joe. Mr Bull, the plumber and Mr Darby, the miller. A rates collector, gravediggers (masons when not on churchyard duty) *and a baker and confectioner, Mr and Mrs Sweeting* (now the Paper Shop). *There was a curious little cottage* (this cottage was up the slope behind Lovells Cottage) *where Mrs Maria Saunders made and sold big peppermint bulls-eyes and, as a supplementary industry, sometimes bought wholesale and sold retail large boxes of bloaters. Certain men were known as reliable hedge trimmers or as good thatchers. There was a village dressmaker - a middle-aged spinster, Miss Gurnett, who went out by day and did all the family mending, charging a shilling a day and her keep. There was of course the doctor, my great uncle Mortimer.*

Harry's father, Leonard Roberts, had made several thousand pounds in a gold rush at Ballarat, Australia whilst still in his teens. He invested his money wisely on returning to England. Still in his early manhood he settled in Bishops Lydeard, married a farmer's daughter and became a retired gentleman. He was buried in the churchyard, on his death in 1895, at the age of 70. It was written at the time: "*a long and a most distressing illness overshadowed the closing years of his life, a great part of which was passed in this village. Mr Robert's removal breaks another of those links with the past, whose severance marks for us the changes of the hands of time.*"

Leonard Roberts was one of the growing 'middle class' at that time. At the bottom of the financial ladder was a farm labourer called Yendell who lived in a cottage in Frog Street - he recounted that: "*my wife, Elizabeth, and I worked all day, I had rheumatism in every joint and there was a period of two years when we didn't see a bit of butcher's meat although we generally had a bit of bacon to boil with turnips on Sunday. My wife didn't allow me to keep poultry or a pig for fear they would tempt me to steal corn from the farm to feed them. My wages at the time (1881) were less than 14 shillings a week.*" Frederick Yendell had eight children to feed!

Yendell and his family were typical of the majority of families in Bishops Lydeard and Cothelstone during the 19th century. As agricultural labourers they worked on the many farms belonging to the Lethbridge and Esdaile estates. The soil produced excellent crops of wheat, beans, barley, mangold, potatoes and turnips. Farming was prosperous enough by 1860 for the formation of the Bishops Lydeard Agricultural Society which lasted nearly 40 years whilst Henry John Pearse was secretary. He was also the registrar of births and deaths of the the village. The society held annual meetings for the distribution of prizes.

Family Fortunes

By the beginning of the 19th century Sir John Lethbridge had enlarged the house at Sandhill Park and added paintings to the walls: Reynolds, Gainsborough, Poussin, and Salvator Rosa. He also increased the size of the estate which his son Sir Thomas, the second baronet, continued doing. By 1825 there were 3984 acres in all consisting of 27 farms, 3 inns, 2 smithies, 2 mills and 100 cottages and shops. The 'Big House' offered employment to those servants within it, and a large staff was needed to maintain the grounds and stables. The financial status of the Lethbridges was important to the economy of the village. It was vital that they not only ran the house but farmed the lands (through tenants) around Bishops Lydeard. Thomas also exercised further control through his parliamentary seat. He was the moral and responsible head of the community, the pioneer of new or improved methods of farming and the provider of better cottages and conditions. Besides the management of the estate, as a landowner, he was expected to act in various capacities, in particular as a magistrate.

Sandhill Park and Mansion c.1830

Reception Hall

Above: The double Drawing - room

Below: Library

Sir Thomas had made a romantic marriage, in 1796, rather than an arranged one. The young lady was Jessie Catherine Hesketh, of Rufford Hall, Lancaster. Thomas had gone up to Lancaster to claim her as his bride but obviously did not have her father's consent. So the impetuous young squire bundled his beloved into a post chaise, and cracking his whip set off with the speed of the wind towards Scotland and matrimony at Gretna Green. Despite the fact that he and his bride-to-be had 75 miles to cover, they obviously succeeded in their quest before the irate father could call out his coach or saddle his horse to start off in pursuit. Legend in the family told of: *"postillions urging on steaming horses and a rumbling coach, in the hurried flight of a happy couple to a small village on the borders of Scotland, remarkable for the clandestine marriages that were celebrated there by an officiating blacksmith."* It is sad that Jesse lived to be only 29 and was buried in 1801 in St Mary's Church, Bishops Lydeard.

Thomas became a Member of Parliament in 1806 - a kind of John Bull character verging on caricature. He once proclaimed: *"you wished me to say what my principles are. I answer in two words - Church and King, by which I mean that it is my intention to make the basis of my political conduct the entire preservation of our glorious establishments, whether of Church or State, the main pillar of which is, in my mind, the Protestant ascendancy in all matters. In order to effect this, as a preliminary indispensable, I certainly shall give, as far as my humble abilities will enable me, the most decided opposition to the admission of Papists to political power."*

Sir Thomas was a generous man in service and equally so in financial help to the villages of Bishops Lydeard and Ash Priors. He was also a sportsman, building a fives wall at the Ale House (The Gore Inn now The Lethbridge Arms) and also patronising cock fighting, wrestling and cudgels there.

His financial benevolence towards the village was matched by his own entrepreneurial activities, investing in an ironworks in South Wales and mining in the Brendon Hills. These activities proved financially disastrous and he died in 1849 leaving debts of £11,221. This was the beginning of the decline of the Sandhill Park estate, as his son, grandson and great-grandson were unable to restore the family fortunes over the next sixty years.

In an effort to improve the family fortunes, Sir John, the third baronet, let Sandhill Park around 1861 to the wealthy Lord Kensington. Sir John himself went to live in Ilfracombe. In 1866 he decided to sell many of the artefacts in the House - which obviously raised several hundred guineas. A little story is told of him whilst he was bearing the consequences of his father's misfortunes, which shows a vein of humour mingled with his serious thoughts. At the level crossing over the railway (Marks Crossing) is the track which led up to the farm, which once stood there, known as Marks after the name of the occupier. When the old man was nearing the end of his days, Sir John paid him a visit one day and, in the course of conversation, said to him: *"Well, Mr Marks, as you will meet my father before I shall, be good enough, if you please, to tell him that Sandhill Park is still not out of debt."*

Sir Wroth, his son, was able to return to Sandhill in 1873. These were days of great life and activity in the house but they were not to last and the sad death of the beautiful Lady Lethbridge and the tragic death of Sir Wroth's second wife left him broken hearted. Sir Wroth's son went on to make an unfortunate first marriage ending in divorce in 1911 and with many debts still facing the estate it was let again, but finally the Sandhill Park Estate was sold in 1913.

With the demise of one estate, another, which had begun in 1831, had risen to take its place by the end of the 19th century.

Winters at Watts

Watts House
c.1850.

The story has been told of the 'Ghost of Coombe Wood' - the irascible John Winter. So what can be said of the family from whence he came and their connection to Watts House (Cedar Falls)?

In a will of a certain John Winter, dated 1715, it is written that he left to his brother Charles: *"a fardel of land of old auster situate and lying and being within the Parish of Bishops Lydeard at or near a place called Watts Bridge containing 20 acres and previously in the tenure of Mary Miles, widow, lately deceased and now in the possession of one Gregory Miles."* ('A fardel' was the term for a small parcel of land and 'old auster' referred to the fact that the land had a roofed house on it). Charles Winter left this same land to his nephew Philip, who never married. So in 1776 he bequeathed Watts to his nephew, Charles.

This Charles Winter was the elder son of his generation and lived in Court House, Ash Priors. In 1755 Charles had married Dorothy Yea and they had four sons, none of whom married. Charles' inheritance from his Uncle Philip made him a wealthy landowner with farms in Lydeard, Cotford, Kingston, Staplegrove and Merridge. (Charles' younger brother, Robert, with obviously no hope of inheriting large sums of money, was sent to Sherborne, Dorset, where he set up as a Mercer, married and had two sons, the elder of whom was named Charles). Charles and Dorothy's second son had inherited Watts's Bridge House by 1799. His name was John - the 'Ghost of Coombe Wood', who began the vendetta with John Lethbridge. The old house was sited by Watts Bridge where the present entrance to Cedar Falls now lies. It had a garden, orchards and fishponds. John Winter eventually died, as has already been said, unmarried, in 1829, leaving an immense amount of property including *"all that tenement called Watts Estate with fish ponds and plantations thereto belonging."*

An interesting report appeared in the local paper in 1809 recording the celebrations for the Jubilee of George III: *"at Court House Mr Thomas Winter began the day by treating the labourers and their families with toast and cider. They then marched to the Church headed by the band. Triumphal arches, royal salutes, beef, pudding and 'October' beer followed. The evening festivities took place at Watts place, where immense bonfires were lit and a fat sheep roasted. There were also illuminations and fireworks".*

In 1829 then, John Winter left the estate to his cousin, Charles, the elder son of Robert Winter of Sherborne mentioned earlier. Charles had married his cousin, Frances Arundell Hanne, from Deviock, near Bodmin, a wealthy lady in her own right. With all this wealth Charles decided to return to his roots and build a large house for himself. It is said that he erected Watts House on the hilltop in order to annoy the Lethbridge's in Sandhill Park by interrupting their view across to the Quantocks - after all the Lethbridge's were newcomers from north Devon compared to the long established Winter's!

The house was completed in 1831 and consisted of a vestibule, breakfast room, study, drawing room, dining room, china pantry, servant's hall, kitchen, scullery, pantry, dairy, cellar, brewhouse, laundry, eight bedrooms, two dressing rooms, stables, coach house and Bartons. The old Watts Bridge house was demolished. Charles died in 1836 apparently never having gone upstairs but living in his library and study.

His elder son, yet another Charles, had been at school at Sherborne and had become a barrister. He lived in London for a time, entering society and Court circles. He became a Gentleman at Arms and a Goldstick-in-waiting to Queen Victoria. Charles, like a great number of the men in the Winter family, never married, and was an eccentric - he always wore white gloves in the house because his hands were supposed to be so beautiful! On his death, in 1864, it was found that the cellars contained nearly 1200 bottles of wine including 24 bottles of 1788 ports. Sale of furniture from the house, by Greenslade of Taunton, lasted three days and raised £1,127.11s. 6d.

The estate went to Charles' sister, Frances, who was unmarried, but a note subsequently found indicated that he had wished it to go to his brother, John. On certain conditions Frances agreed and Lynchfield House was bought for her. John was not physically very strong and with his health failing he took a sea trip to South Africa. However he died at Lagoa Bay in 1873, aged 51, and his body was brought back to Bishops Lydeard to be buried in the churchyard alongside other members of the family.

His son, John Arundell Winter, was a Major in the army in 1873 and had little desire to live at Watts House, besides which he was not a good money manager. He placed the following advert in the Times of 21st August 1873:

'Somersetshire, in the Parish of Bishops Lydeard five miles from the county town of Taunton, and one from the Bishops Lydeard railway station, on the West Somerset branch of the Bristol and Exeter railway. A first class residence and 79 acres of superior land, with or without the shooting over, upwards of 1000 acres, containing good preserves and well stocked with game: - to be LET, unfurnished, from Michaelmas next, for a term of three, five, or seven years, the delightful mansion known as Watts House, containing spacious entrance hall, noble and large dining and drawing rooms, breakfast room, library, study, 14 bed and dressing rooms, ample and most convenient domestic offices, with extensive underground cellars, good stabling, carriage houses, harness room, sheds for cows, pigs and poultry, first-rate walled garden, flower garden, conservatory, Orchard House, stocked with choice fruit trees in full bearing. The house has a southern aspect, standing on an elevation, from which may be obtained splendid views of the surrounding country, and is approached from the South Lodge by a carriage drive winding through a fine timbered Park, containing fish ponds and pleasure gardens, and which must be seen to be appreciated. The lands comprise rich meadow, orchard, and arable land, all in a high state of cultivation, and the whole or any part may be taken with the house, and with or without the shooting. The above residence is within reach of the Devon and Somerset Staghounds, Mr Luttrell's Fox Hounds and different packs of Harriers hunt in the neighbourhood. On view on Tuesdays, Wednesdays and Thursdays from 11am to 4pm, by cards only, which may be obtained of Mr Greenslade, auctioneer, steward and land surveyor, at his offices in Trull and Taunton, of whom terms of letting and all other particulars may be obtained.'

The estate was let to a Mr Tilney for the sum of £380 per annum.

Major Arundell Winter was a man with a fierce temper and, as has been indicated, a spendthrift. This temper drove his children across the world - the boys to Africa, California, Malaya and Argentina and one of the girls to Africa and the other, Marjorie, to Sweden and Russia. Marjorie was locked up by the revolution forces in Petrograd (Leningrad) and accused of spying. She was sentenced to be shot, but was fortunately released after about a year. Major

Winter obviously had no qualms about the feud with the Lethbridge's because he agreed, in 1873, to exchange Court House, the old family home, together with other land, for land near Watts House belonging to Sir Wroth Lethbridge.

As a result of his high style of living and lack of financial acumen, Major Winter found he could not afford to keep the estate and so he sold it in 1891 to Major Ashford Lovatt Wise for £14,750. In 1902 Watts House and estate was sold again for £19,000 to Dennis Boles, of whom more will be written later.

The Parochial School

The lives of most Victorian children in Bishops Lydeard centered around the school when they were not working in the fields. The Parochial School was funded by voluntary subscriptions from around 1850 with a schoolmaster or mistress in charge. Staff did not stay long in the post - Robert Cooksley (1860), Frederick Borough (1865), Miss Beamer (1871).

Following lengthy arguments over the choice of site, building and financial wranglings and religious disagreements, a new school was started on 1st April 1872 and used for the first time on 20th December 1872. It consisted of one main stone block partitioned into classroom areas and a house for the schoolmaster and his wife, who at the time were Walter Pugh with his wife as the sewing mistress. The school had a capacity of 200 children but the average attendance was rarely above 130.

The logbook records that in 1875 the Vicar, Rev Murray Mathew, refused to teach the first class because of the bad behaviour of the *'big girls'*. On another occasion when a boy was sent to the Headmaster for punishment, the boy refused to be beaten and *'taking his hat, he left the school'*. The fluctuations in attendance were often recorded as due to *'gleaning not having been finished, the whortleberry season starting, haymaking in full swing, and pheasant beating in Sandhill Park'*. There were also many illnesses to disrupt school life, one of the most common recorded being *'fever'*. During a bout of 'brain fever' (possibly meningitis) in 1884 the Headmaster, Mr Tremellan, wrote *'parents are complaining of the pressures which we are obliged to put on the children in order to get their work done, as being injurous to both body as well as the brains of their children'*. On the same page he records, *'Annie P died this week, the brain being infected'*.

Until 1891 children had to pay each week for their tuition and a lot of absence was caused due to objections over charges. The charges were 'labourers one penny, better classes two pence'. By 1897 some contributions were still being made as the Headmaster, Mr Simons, wrote, *'the school has five scholars paying four pence weekly. A better class of children I find are now gradually making their way to school'*. Mr Simons was responsible for paying all the school expenditure, including the £14 annual salary to the student teachers.

Mr Tremellan had sadly died at the age of 36 in 1883, and Mr C.F. Simons was appointed, from Stockland School near Honiton, and took up the post in the June of that year. Mr Simons continued until his death in September 1913 and a poem was written by Elizabeth Clarke (Sir Arthur C. Clarke's grandmother) at the time:

Our Schoolmaster

We see his kindly smile no more,
We miss his many deeds of love,
For now his earthly work is o'er
And God has taken him above.

His gentleness and patience mild,
Are ever in our memory clear,
For in the heart of every child,
His influence lives for ever dear.

That influence which will never die,
The poorly we can it define,
Shines clear before the Heavenly Eye,
For it's akin to the divine.

Oh God, who knowest every heart,
Thou knowest his life was not in vain,
In very truth he did his part,
But not for earthly praise nor gain.

'Twas natural for him day by day,
In kindly thoughtfulness to rule,
His words will never fade away,
With pleasure we remember school.

His face so calm, yet full of power
We fain would see: God knowest best.
He is at peace for ever more,
In that bright home of perfect rest.

School finances were always precarious, in May 1882 the Annual Report of the School Committee stated that, 'the school was £17.11.11$^{1}/_{4}$d in debt, which was over £13 better than the previous year'! It asked for subscribers to pay their subscriptions six months earlier so that the school did not run on borrowed money. Mr Tremellan volunteered to take a £10 cut in his salary. This would be unheard of today!!

Her Majesty's Inspectors inspected the school each year and their report of November 1881 said that, *'Mr and Mrs Tremellan and the staff came out with great credit. It was regretted that so many children leave when they get to the fifth standard.'* It also impressed upon parents the importance of sending their children regularly to school, *'as it is impossible for the best masters to make good scholars out of irregular ones.'* Of the pupils it was reported that, *'they have passed a highly creditable exam in reading, writing and arithmetic, the paperwork of the upper standard deserving praise in particular on account of its general neatness and accuracy'*.

A Diary of Village Entertainment - Victorian Style

Christmas 1881: The children of Bishops Lydeard were reminded that Christmas was a time for mirth and gladness. Nearly all the children saw a Magic Lantern Show put on by Mr and Mrs Tilney (from Watts House). Some of the wonders they saw, bringing forth round after round of applause, were views of London and the Continent, John Gilpin on his never to be forgotten ride, an old man with and without umbrellas, flowers in full bloom and a rat eater who never seemed satisfied! Simple pleasures in comparison with modern entertainment.

Mr Bissett M.P. and Cecil Smith Esq. (Lydeard House) gave trees to the Sunday School children which were decorated with candles. Prizes of popguns, dolls, trumpets, sweetmeats and woollen materials were distributed according to attendance and marks obtained during the year.

Wednesday 9th August 1882: The Annual School and Sunday School Treat. On a lovely sunny afternoon at 3 pm the children marched to the Church with their banners. After a short service they marched to Vicarage Field, provided by Mr Alfred Skinner, for a tea and did ample justice to all the good things provided for them. With tea over, various games were played with a will and when evening came the most deserving children were presented with a little gift from the Vicar. Teachers and visitors had tea on the vicarage lawn and the church bells were rung.

December 1882: It was decided to alleviate the chill and routine of winter's evenings for the poorer and less well-educated people who did not have the benefit of a bright fire, comfortable room, books and music, by providing Penny Entertainment in the schoolroom. Cecil Smith Esq., C.E.J. Esdaile Esq. (Cothelstone House) and Mr and Mrs Tilney presided over the entertainment of readings, music and singing at a cost of one penny to enter. Penny Entertainment went on throughout that winter and each winter certainly until the end of the century.

Thursday 8th January 1885: A concert was held to raise funds to help pay off the debt on the Coffee Tavern. Tickets were available from the Tavern priced 2/-, 1/- and 6d. [Mr M. Fenwick Bissett M.P. had opened a Coffee Tavern on 29th October 1881 after the Ladies Boarding School, run by Miss Edney, closed down. This Tavern and previously School were in Birch House beside the Paper Shop].

Thursday 27th August 1885: A 'Bazaar' was held at Lynchfield House (now Dunkirk Memorial House). The committee, set up in April, had decided this was a good day being a Taunton half-holiday and an extra afternoon and evening train was running. The Bazaar was opened at 2 pm by the Hon. Mrs Stanley (the wife of the local M.P.) and entertainment was provided by Prince Albert's Somerset Light Infantry Military Band. Amusements during the afternoon were an Aunt Sally, quoits, Punch and Judy and many stalls. The proceeds went to provide heating for the Church and the enlargement of the Vestry.

Tuesday 21st June 1887: The Golden Jubilee of Queen Victoria was celebrated by a large procession, headed by a band and the Vicar, to the Church. A dinner was held for the men, whilst the women and children had tea. The remainder of the day was spent with athletic sports and dancing.

1st May 1888: The first match of the newly formed Bishops Lydeard Cricket Club was played.

8th August 1889: The first Bishops Lydeard & District Flower Show was held at Watts House.

July 1893: The Royal Wedding of Prince George, Duke of York, and Princess Victoria May of Teck. This event, of great national interest and importance, was very happily observed in Bishops Lydeard. The long procession of school children with their flags and flowers, led by the village band, was a pretty sight as it made its way to Lydeard House, where, as guests of G. Saunders Esq. and Mrs Saunders, the young folk sat down to a good tea. With the subscriptions placed at their disposal, the committee provided a good meat tea for the over sixties. Under the direction of Dr Frossard some well-arranged athletics were held, which afforded much amusement to the large company assembled, as well as some profit to the competitors. A pretty effect was produced by many coloured lights, provided by Mr Saunders, and shown just before 'good night' was said.

In 1859 money was being sought as plans had been drawn up to increase the size of the Church by adding the north aisle. Money was a continuing problem for next 35 years and by 1894 the Organ Fund was occupying most attention. It appears that parishioners were not too forthcoming with their contributions and urgent appeals for support were being made by the Vicar, Rev Eustace.

What he wrote at the time gives an interesting account of the numbers of villagers involved in promoting community activities.

Thursday 26th July 1894: 'The Fancy Fair was a very pleasing remembrance, particularly in the form of a deposit at Messrs. Stuckey's Bank to the value of £67. First of all we were under the deepest obligation to the gentleman spoken of as the 'Clerk of the Weather'. On Tuesday the outlook was so gloomy that we hardly liked to think, much less to speak of, the prospect for our Fair, but when Thursday came we could not have wished a better day. The pretty grounds of Lydeard House looked their best. Nowhere else would we have had so many attractions on offer. In this instance the picture gained by its framing : the well-filled fancy stalls were presided over by Mrs Eustace, Mrs Foster, Mrs Saunders, Mrs Fligg, the Misses Saunders, Mr and Mrs Worrall, Miss Turner and Miss Edwards. The Refreshment Stall by Mrs and Misses Skinner. The Flower Stall by Mrs Smith and Mrs Le Measurer. The Advertisement Stall by Miss Follett and Mrs Burston. The Fairy Well by Miss E. Skinner. Drs. Frossard and Fligg, Messrs Skinner, Saunders, Simons, Trickey, Bull, Clarke, Lamson, Ruddle, Newton, Northcombe, Upham, Barber, Ashman, Dauncey and Barnscott kindly directed the many amusements and acted as stewards. Mrs Crease with her waxworks attracted large audiences. The Messrs. Saunders with their boat had a very busy time.

The Fair was opened by Mrs Wilfred Marshall. The Bishops Lydeard Band very kindly gave their services, which were highly appreciated, to Bandmaster Tarr and the members of his band we were much indebted. Mr Skinner, our long-serving Churchwarden, thanked Mr and Mrs Saunders for throwing open the grounds of Lydeard House.
The Organ Fund afterwards stood at £270.
At a meeting on 21st March 1895 it was decided to order the organ from Messrs Brindley & Foster of Sheffield and London, at a cost of £500. The fund stood at £339 and events and subscriptions had to continue to the end of the century to meet the costs.

22nd June 1897: The 60 year reign of Queen Victoria was duly celebrated in the Village. A short service was the first feature of the local celebration. Then followed a dinner, tea and various amusements in the grounds of Lydeard House. A day of thorough enjoyment and innocent recreation left pleasant memories for young and old.

Have I got News for You

To complete the tales from the Victorian Years a quick look at the newspapers of the time gives a few more interesting stories:
14th July 1888. A lad from Bishops Lydeard appeared to have gone temporarily insane from sunstroke. He had been caught throwing stones at homes saying, "I'll kill the lot - I killed 500 yesterday."

16th May 1891. Miss Louisa Gardiner of Lynchfield House presented four beautiful cathedral lamps to the Bishops Lydeard Church. They are executed in brass and considerably beautify the appearance of the chancel.
Louisa's mother, Frances, died later that year. She had lived in Lynchfield House for well over thirty years. It was written of her: *she will be a great loss to the Parish. During the many years that she lived here, she was always a kind friend to the poor and a ready and generous supporter of all parochial institutions. Spared to 'a good old age', her long and useful life came to a peaceful end on the morning of 7th December, aged 83.*
The following June in 1892: *the past month has been marked by the departure from our Parish of the Misses Gardner whom we feel sure will be missed by many and in many ways. During a long residence, the Miss Gardiner's were active and zealous church workers. That the work thus done was appreciated by the parishioners was shown by the presents the Misses Gardiner were asked to accept. To mark their sense of Miss Louisa Gardiner's kindness in playing the organ for so many years, the parishioners asked her acceptance of a silver teapot, tea-caddy and kettle, whilst the members of the choir gave her a prayer book. The Sunday School children gave both sisters an inkstand. A large number of the poor, in whose welfare Miss Gardiner was*

much interested, presented her with a prayer book and a copy of the Christian Year.

13th June 1891: A butcher's boy from Bishops Lydeard died from blood poisoning after cutting a finger ten days earlier as he killed a bullock. Tetanus had set into the wound, and the man had worked until the day before his death, not realising the seriousness of the infection.

25th July 1891: Nearly 1000 farmers attended the auction sale of the famous herd of Devon cattle, belonging to Alfred Skinner, at Pound Farm. He had won no less than 237 prizes since 1890, the highest being that of the Jubilee Gold Cup, which was presented to him by Her Majesty Queen Victoria.

21st November 1891: An appeal was made by a member of the public to reopen an ancient footpath, closed by the previous owners, across Phiffin Meadows to Lynchfield. It is said that in Phiffin Lane (note original spelling) there was an ancient bishop's palace, with niches in the porch for holy water. (The 'palace' concerned in Piffin Lane was the vicarage).

27th May 1893: A meeting on the 25th May was held in the schoolroom at Bishops Lydeard, attended by the canvassers, for the purpose of presenting their reports on the lighting of the town. Sufficient funds of £42.7.0d were promised to carry out the work, which has long been necessary. A committee were elected to carry out the work and make the arrangements for the lighting for the ensuing winter.
In September: *the arrangements are nearly complete and, before the month closes, the lamps will cast their rays as we hope to the comfort and greater safety of all who have to walk our alas so ill-kept village street. Why, at least, the original footpath, traces of which are to be seen, should not be kept in proper order, more than one ratepayer would be glad to know? Why not lay our grievance before the County Council? Something ought to be done. The £40 promised has been expended in the purchase and erection of the lamps now in place.*

7th January 1894. Ice Spectacle: At Bishops Lydeard, the Sandhill Pond is thickly frozen over, skating being much enjoyed by a large number of visitors. On Monday night, a large company of skaters enjoyed this agreeable exercise by moonlight and, on Thursday, there were about 200 skaters with torches and Chinese lanterns presenting a most animated appearance. The Bishops Lydeard Band performed on both occasions.

Edwardian
Bishops
Lydeard

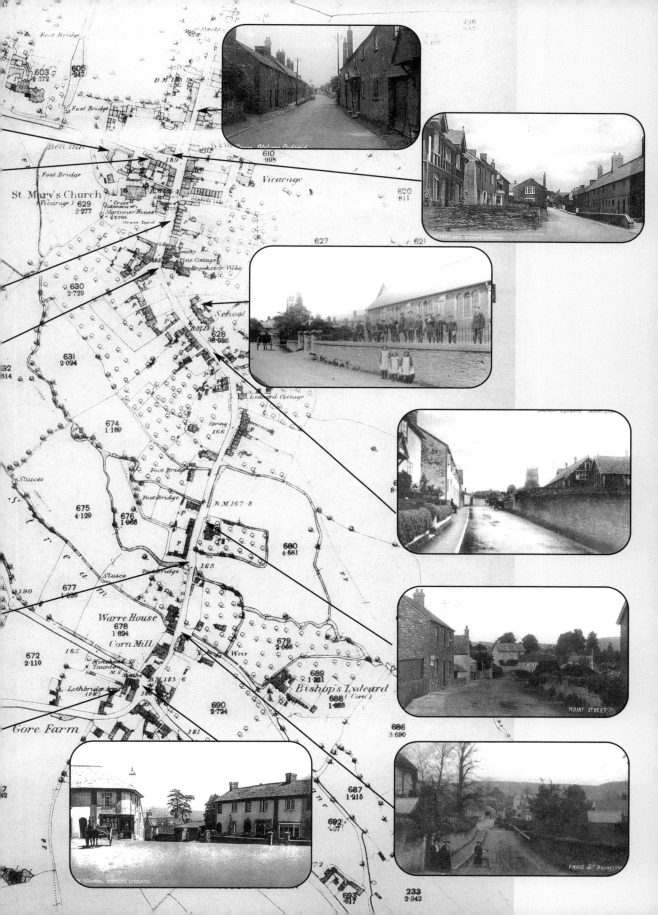

Watts House
1902
The house before being enlarged by Sir Dennis Boles.
The Cedar Tree is some seventy years old by this time.

— Five —
Watts Behind the Name ?

Dennis Boles

Hastings Fortesque Boles

Gerald Boles

Watts House

Upstairs, Downstairs

Connaught House School

Cedar Falls

Whats Behind the Name?
Dennis Boles

*Colonel
Sir Dennis Boles*

Dennis's father had been born in Crowcombe and became the vicar there. So Dennis was brought up in the West country and the country life influenced his enjoyment of hunting, shooting and fishing. He was able to pursue these sports and buy Watts House and the estate because he married the eldest daughter of the steel magnate, John Lycett - Lycett Steel of Bristol, who was reputed to have an emerald collection second only to the late Queen Mother. John Lycett also was the only man to have swum the channel and play on the Centre Court at Wimbledon, taking a set off Fred Perry. Beatrice Ringrose Lycett and Dennis Boles had five children - Hastings, Violet, Doreen, Gerald and Nesta. As a young man Dennis entered military service, which he finally left in 1917 as commander of the 3rd Battalion Devonshire Regiment. His eldest son, Hastings, was killed during the Great War. Dennis received the CBE in 1919.

He became MP for West Somerset in 1911 and was re-elected in 1918 for the newly formed Taunton Division. In 1922 he took the Chiltern Hundreds,* because he had been created a baronet for his public services.

In 1923 Sir Dennis became High Sheriff of Somerset. He was a man of unbounded energy and never spared himself in the service of others. The loftiness of his ideals and the unselfishness of his character made giving a pleasure. He was a very devout churchman and the beauty of the chancel in Bishops Lydeard Church and the window in the south aisle, is due to the generosity of Lady Beatrice and

*Lady Beatrice
Boles*

himself, having the work done in memory of their eldest son and of the other members of the Parish who gave their lives for their country.

Sir Dennis suffered from angina and, in 1935, during the Puppy Show, held each year on the cricket field, he collapsed and died. Lady Beatrice lived until the spring of 1939, although during the last seven years of her life, she was confined to a wheelchair with arthritis.

An MP could apply for the Chiltern Hundreds which gave him stewardship of a district (formerly called a hundred) which includes part of the Chiltern Hills and is Crown property, and hence to be allowed to resign his seat, since the holding of an office of profit under the Crown disqualifies him from being an MP.

The Boles Family c.1912

Left to right :
Gerald, Doreen, Hastings,
Lady Beatrice with Nesta,
and Violet.

Dennis Boles (back seat)
on the campaign trail.

Haymaking at Watts 1904.

Left. Sir Dennis with his first four children. 1904

Left. Sir Dennis with both the Quantock and West Somerset hounds, painted by Alfred Haig. The painting now resides in a Californian Bank.

Bottom Left. Sir Dennis being presented with the painting at the 1929 Puppy Show.

Below. The last photograph of Sir Dennis. He collapsed and died several minutes after it had been taken. 1935.

Hastings Fortesque Boles

2nd Lieutenant Hastings Boles of the 17th Lancers.

Hastings was the elder son of Sir Dennis. He was born on 21st June 1895 and educated at Evelyn's, West Drayton, Eton and Sandhurst. He was gazetted to the 17th Lancers on 16th December 1914, receiving his commission in January 1915. By March he was attached to the Royal Flying Corps as an Observation Officer and soon joined the Expeditionary Force in France.

Hastings was a good all round sportsman, a keen fisherman and cricketer. He was passionately fond of music, being himself a remarkable performer as he played entirely by ear. He was always ready to use his great gift to give pleasure to others and when off duty was the source of much entertainment for his brother officers and men.

Hastings was ordered to photograph behind enemy lines, which was a difficult and hazardous task. However when he had identified the area for photographing he was as quick as lightning and took the photographs at such a rate that the pilot had no need to turn and go over the ground again.

His commanding officer wrote to Sir Dennis:

"The results he obtained were of the best the Flying Corps has produced. Photography of German trenches is of tremendous value and the results of his work were of great value indeed to our army. Only the day before his death he had been up photographing and on his return showed me the back of his hand, which had been grazed by an anti-aircraft splinter. He laughed at it. I am having those last photographs he took which showed the anti-aircraft shell actually fired at the machine, bursting beneath, as well as the country he was ordered to take, redone so as to send to you, when this war is over, as they are splendid examples of his skill and bravery. On the day he was wounded your son was making an ordinary reconnaissance. He was very gallant and an example to us all."

The pilot, who was with Lieutenant Boles when he was wounded, wrote:

"I feel I must let you know how splendidly he acted after being wounded. When in the air he looked back and smiled, at the time waving to let me know he was all right. On the ground he would not allow us to lift him from the machine, but got out himself."

Sadly Hastings died of wounds at Bailleul in France on 24th May 1915. He was just 19 years of age. However it is clear that in the three months he served in the RFC he had made a tremendous impression on those around him.

At 3pm on 1st June 1915 a Memorial Service was held in Bishops Lydeard Church. The Bishop of Taunton during his address paid the following tribute to Hastings Fortesque Boles:

"A young man, full of promise, a boy with grit, go and pluck; one who was not afraid to go in the air over enemy lines; one who could keep his head, and one who was ready to use his gifts for others delight as well as his own, as we hear from the front that he did with his gift of music. He was one who had that presence of mind and pluck which we so often admire in our men."

On the following two pages is reproduced the story of Hastings Boles in his RFC plane over the lines, from the 'Victor' comic of 1982. His name has been spelt Hoskins Boles.

Hasting's grave in Bailleul, France.

Gerald Boles

Sir Gerald and Lady Violet Blanche Boles

The wedding of Gerald and Blanche in Kensington.

Mr. Gerald Fortescue Boles, 17th/21st Lancers, only surviving son of Sir Dennis Boles, was married last week to Miss Violet Blanche Hall Parlby, elder daughter of Major and Mrs. Hall Parlby, at St. Mary Abbot's, Kensington.

As Hastings had been killed, on Sir Dennis's death his second son, Gerald, became the second baronet. Gerald had married Violet Blanche Hall Parlby, in 1927 and went out to Bermuda as ADC to the Governor. On his return to this country he decided to study horticulture and settled in Cirencester, where his son Jeremy was conceived. Jeremy was born in Marylebone, London but the family finally returned to Somerset to Stonehouse at Hele, Bradford-on-Tone. After Lady Beatrice's death, Gerald, Blanche and Jeremy moved into Watts House, just before the outbreak of war. They had not been there long before one night Sir Gerald rang up Watts House from London and said to Blanche, "You have 36 hours to get to Liverpool. You're booked on a boat to Canada and from there the 'Lady Summers' will take you down to Jack Lycett's villa at Cable Beach in Nassau. So Jeremy and Blanche spent the war in the Bahamas. Sir Gerald had been in North Africa with the American forces but joined Monty's caravan and was with Montgomery through North Africa, Tunisia, Sicily and on into Italy. He was working as a censor in Bari when an American ammunition ship blew up just outside his office and he was killed. He was identified by a soldier who happened to have been a porter on Bishops Lydeard railway station.

Jeremy, at the age of 12, had now become the third baronet and he and his mother, Blanche, returned in 1944, on the Mauritania from New York to Southampton. She rented Fennington Farm and on 30th October 1945 Blanche married David Carver, whom she had met during the war in the Bahamas. Sir Jeremy was sent to Connaught House School, which had been relocated to Watts House during the war. It was most strange for the young baronet to be at school in the house which he owned!

A young Sir Jeremy Boles with his grandfather, Dennis, and Mr Worral at the Puppy Show.

It was also difficult for Randall Hoyle, the headmaster, as Jeremy knew where things were in the house. He did not know whether to beat the boy for breaking into things or let him get away with it! Sir Jeremy sold Watts House to Randall Hoyle in 1964.

Watts House

Originally, on entering the house through the front door there was a small inner hall and then a back hall from which the staircase went up. On the right of the hall there was a small dining room and on the left-hand side the drawing room beyond which was a study and beyond again a small second study.

Sir Dennis enlarged the house by building on a music room, as Lady Beatrice was a very good musician, and installed an organ. He had the family crest put into the stained-glass windows at one end. On the right of the hall, beyond the dining room, Sir Dennis built on another room which became the dining room and beyond that he built a billiard room and library, with leather library chairs along the wall, and finally there was a gun room. During the war all the books were taken from the library to one of the garages, where the estate lorry was kept. Unfortunately the floor was not waterproof and nearly all the books had to be destroyed after eight years in the damp.

Staircase in Watts House

The drawing-room remains but the original dining room is now part of the main hall of Cedar Falls. The gun room and old Butler's pantry have been incorporated into the present kitchens. Where the boutique complex is now situated was the old kitchen and the hair salon was the Servants Hall. Treatment rooms for the health spa are now in the old cellars.

Entrance Hall after the alterations by Sir Dennis. The part of the hall with the fireplace was the dining room of the original house.

Drawing - room at Watts House

Boating on the Lower Pond

The Ponds 1904

The Fishpond

The gardens of Watts House were extremely lovely. On the south side of the house was the large enclosed rose garden in the middle of which was a large circular goldfish pond with a fountain. The overflow from this pond was carried by a lead pipe down into the stream which meandered through the rock garden which Gerald, using his horticultural skills, designed. (This rock garden and the bed of the stream are still visible amongst the trees, by the 3rd Tee of the golf course). The stream ended in a waterfall which fell into a large pond below and then on into the top lake. The top lake was filled with around 250 to 500 trout each year by Exmoor fisheries. They used the lake as a stew pond and the family were allowed to take out so many fish each year. The pond was lowered to allow stock to be taken out for spawning and as the water level dropped a lot of eels were also caught. All three lakes were used for boating, the boat being stored in a small boathouse beside the middle pond.

The water for the gardens was supplied by a 'ram' situated above East Combe Farmhouse which pumped the water up to a reservoir above the farm. The water was then fed by gravity to all the taps in the greenhouses, gardens and stables. It was also used to feed the house until the mains water supply was connected from Bagborough.

Above left. The old carpenter's sheds on which were built the flats, seen above right.

The original Fishpond fountain can still be seen in the foreground.

Situated where the flats have now been built were a range of sheds - potting sheds, sheds for the carpenters and plumbers and beyond the rose garden were the magnificent greenhouses.

Watts House had three walled gardens. The first, surrounded by a stone wall, was situated where the outdoor swimming pool now is. A second garden, again surrounded by a stone wall, was situated beyond and the main walled garden was entered through a gate from this. This garden had a grass cross with rose pergolas that outlined the shape and in the centre of the cross was a bird bath. There was a path around the brick built walls on which there were cordons of apples, peaches, pears and nectarines. On the north-facing wall there were red and white currants. In front of you, on the left, was a large bed of gooseberries and on the right there were strawberries. In other plots there were lilies of the valley as well as the many vegetables grown for the house. To the east of the gardens,

Above. The magnificent Cedar tree before the conversion of Watts House into the present day Health Farm, Cedar Falls.

The coach house and stables.

The Boles Family transport.

On the following pages are photographs from Lady Beatrice Bole's photograph album showing the Rock Garden and the Rose Garden in 1928.

Rock Garde

1929

Rose Ga

Watts House 1928

surrounded by the hedges, were four grass tennis courts and beyond, where the car park now is, was the hard tennis court. To the north is the cricket ground. This was dug out and levelled by hand, using just a horse and cart to move the soil. The front of the house is dominated by the superb cedar tree which, at the time of writing, is some 170 years old.

Upstairs, Downstairs

Sir Dennis employed thirty two staff during the first three decades of the last century. In the house there were the butler, two footmen, cook, kitchen maid, housemaids and parlour maids. Outside there were gardeners, grooms, chauffeurs, carpenters, dairy maids, cowman, gamekeeper and others skilled in caring for the land and animals on the estate, supervised by the estate agent, Mr Kitson.

In the early years, Sir Dennis had up to eleven grooms to look after his thirty six coach horses and hunters. These were housed around the stable yard - five loose boxes facing north and the covered boxes facing south with the hay loft above. Also in the loft were the mills for rolling oats and the chaff-cutters, all driven by electricity from a generator turned by water power from the lakes. The head groom was Alfred Shepherd, who taught Sir Jeremy to ride. The dairy was also off the yard, and in it all the butter and cream for the house was made, from the milk produced by the herd of Guernsey cows .

Later, of course, chauffeurs replaced many of the grooms as the 'horseless carriage' took over - the early cars comprised a Minerva saloon and Talbot and Sunbeam open tops. The roads in those days were mostly dirt tracks and the cars always returned very dirty. They were thoroughly washed before work for the day was finished - this included removing the wheels to clean the underside. The head chauffeur was Fred James. Many of the men were survivors of the Great War and some had resulting health problems. Nearly all, however, smoked, rolling their own cigarettes - Woodbines were five for tuppence (1p).

Sir Dennis built Knapp Cottages at East Combe, overlooking, to the west, the main road and the steam railway from Taunton to Minehead. In these cottages were housed Shepherd, head groom, James, head chauffeur, and Tuffin, head gardener. The laundry was also at Knapp. Waygood, the assistant head gardener, lived in the Front Lodge. Whitemore, head mason and carpenter, lived in the white thatched Watts Cottage on the bend in the road, outside the gates. Westcombe, carpenter and maintenance man, lived in Watersmeet Cottage just off the main road - he had the privilege of making Sir Dennis's coffin out of oak with an elm lining.

The West Lodge was built on the back drive for the butler, Burgess. He was a tremendous character, always immaculately turned out in his morning suit. Most mornings a little ritual was played out. Burgess would let Sir Dennis ring three times before taking up his shaving water and would always have a convincing

Above : Grooms and Chauffeurs.
On the far left, standing, is Alfred Shepherd (Head Groom), in the middle at the back is Fred James (Head Chauffeur).

Below : Downstairs staff and Gardeners.
Fifth from the left, standing, is Sam Burgess (Butler). The Cook, Miss Alcock, is in the centre with the House and Parlourmaids either side. On the end, in black, is probably Nanny Bater. The Boles girls never went to school, they were taught by governesses. Nanny Bater died at Watts House of cancer.

Above : Cricket at Watts c. 1904
Far right, Sir Dennis and seated, with glasses, Dr Aveline.(from Cotford).

Below : The Homeguard at Watts House. c. 1940
Back row from the left : Whitemore, Tuffin, T. Symonds, H. Rogers,
G. Milton, A. Symonds.
Front row : F. James, S. Burgess, Sir G. Boles, R. Kitson, A. Shepherd.

reply to the question, "Where have you been, Burgess?"

Many garden parties were held in the summer on the cricket field. Another of Burgess's ruses would be to come out of the pavilion with a tray full of drinks and pretend to trip just as he came up to Sir Dennis, always making him jump - considering Sir Dennis's heart condition this probably was not a good idea!

Between the wars, Somerset County Cricket Club used to play Gentlemen and Players matches at Watts House. At one such match Jack White, England and Somerset, had just returned from a successful tour of Australia and was bowling for the Players against the Gentleman's side, got together by Sir Dennis. Burgess, who had a very good eye for hitting a cricket ball, was batting. He dispatched the first two balls from White for six each, whereupon Sir Dennis is reported to have walked up to Burgess and quietly had a word in his ear, "I think you had better give Mr White a little more respect, Burgess, after all he is an England cricketer." So acting on these instructions, he respectfully sent the remaining four balls of the over for just four runs each!

Top:
Tennis party.

Bottom:
The start of a
partridge shoot.

In the hunting and shooting season, house parties would be invited down for a week. As a guest you would say if you were hunting or shooting the next day, and the appropriate clothes would be laid out for you. One could hunt for six days or shoot for four days in a week or a combination of both. During the summer months there would also be private tennis and cricket parties. Two of the most notable visitors, apart from the famous cricketers of the era, were Sir Winston Churchill and Lord Baden-Powell.

Left:
A motorcycle rally

West Somerset Fox Hounds at Watts House. 1904.

Sir Dennis Boles on Comethrow. 1904.

Sir Dennis's hunting record is unique. At his death he had been Master of the West Somerset Foxhounds for 31 years. In 1917, in order to keep down down the deer in a sporting and humane manner, he started the Quantock Staghounds. The Liberal War Cabinet issued a grant and the Controller of Food agreed to buy four horses, ten couple of hounds, pay the wages of two men (Charlie and Fred Taylor) and horse and hound feed for a season. The deer would also provide another source of meat. Shortly after the War, Sir Dennis started the Quantock Foxhound pack and he was then responsible for simultaneously organising two packs of foxhounds and one of staghounds. In the breeding of hounds, the puppies stayed with their mothers until they were eight weeks old, then they were given to local farmers and others, who supported the hunt, to act as 'Puppy Walkers'. For a year they reared the puppies teaching them not to chase sheep, poultry, cats and generally to have good discipline, before being returned to the kennels. At the end of the season the Puppy Show was held, on the cricket field, for the year old hounds. The show would be attended by 300 - 400 people standing three or four deep around the show ring. It was at this show, in 1935, that Sir Dennis died.

Below : The Puppy Show, Watts House.

Inset : Gerald, Doreen, Hastings and Violet with the puppies at the Cannington kennels.

Connaught House School

Connaught House School was a preparatory school for 86 boys, aged 11-13, in Weymouth. At the outbreak of war the school premises were commandeered for barracks by the War Office. The school was moved to Watts House, since Sir Gerald had moved his family to Nassau. A few weeks after the relocation of the school, the War Office announced that it wanted Watts House. However the local MP, Colonel Wickham, finally persuaded the War Office otherwise and the school remained.

Randall Hoyle was the headmaster and he had rooms in house for his wife, Griselda, (known as Grizzle by the boys) and his two children. Mrs Joint was the matron, Paul Cooper was the assistant head, who lived in Frog House in the village, and Miss Mosely (Miss Mo) was Randall Hoyle's secretary. She moved into the Front Lodge. Still known as Mo, at the time of writing she continues to live in the village. Other staff lived in Knapp cottages. Mr Clutterbuck, who was in charge of sports and a Scoutmaster, was adored by the boys. He ran cricket, rugby and soccer teams - the tennis courts becoming a cricket field and soccer pitch and even the front lawn was made into a small cricket field.

Randall Hoyle divided the drawing room into two classrooms, the gun room, billiard room, music room and the groom's rest room were also made into classrooms. Upstairs the bedrooms were made into seven dormitories, a sick bay, matron's room and to the right of the stairs Randall Hoyle's private rooms. The dormitories were named after local hunts, such as Blackmoor Vale, Cattistock, Quantock and Portman. A swimming pool was built by the school in the first walled garden.

Violet Boles had two sons, Simon and Nick. Nick is seen here in his Connaught House School uniform.

Nick Bucknall tells the tale of the time when his brother, Simon, and Jeremy Boles, obtained the key to the wine cellar from Burgess and proceeded to enjoy a bottle from the cellar. After all it was Jeremy's wine so he felt he had a right to it! The headmaster thought otherwise and both lads were given a beating.

Around 1949, Nick also recalls the arrival of a very attractive assistant matron. She had lovely red hair. Unfortunately she found one of the senior boys irresistible and the inevitable happened! To avoid a scandal she left after one term at the school.

Sir Jeremy sold Watts House to Randall Hoyle in 1964 and two years later he retired and Dick Blackley, who was from Ireland, became headmaster. Unfortunately the school started to go downhill, the results went down and so did pupil numbers. At that time the M4 was being

P. S. C. Cooper   R. H. Blackley
S. J. Parkes : W. R. Nixon : A. H. Channer : C. D. Ricardo : R. W. V. Mackintosh : G. N. O. Dolphin : A. M. D. Smallwood
T. F. K. Miller :   J. C. Clothier :   E. P. White : R. W. Morgan : P. M. McComas :
J. B. A. Slade : J. S. Colvin :   E. J. Littleton :   A. P. B. Asher
Played 7 : Won 5 : Lost 1 : Drawn 1 :

Rugby Football Team.
1958.

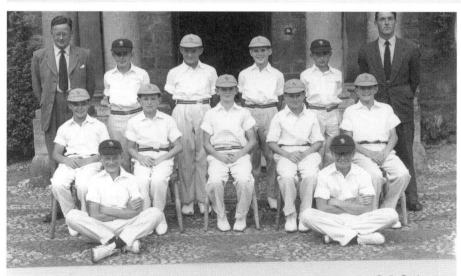

R. H. Blackley : R. N. T. Short : A. R. Nixon : J. C. Clothier : R. J. Bailey :   P. D. Gilbert
E. J. Littleton : R. W. V. Mackintosh : P. M. McComas : A. P. B. Asher : A. H. Channer :
G. C. Forestier Walker   A. M. D. Smallwood
Played 8 : Won 1, Drawn 2, Lost 5 :

Cricket Team.
1959.

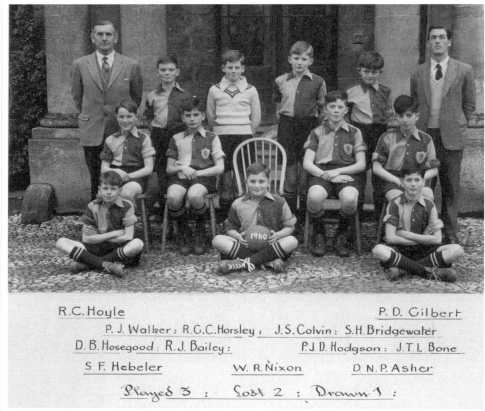

R.C. Hoyle   P. D. Gilbert
P. J. Walker : R.G.C. Horsley ; J.S. Colvin : S.H. Bridgewater
D. B. Hosegood : R.J. Bailey :   P.J.D. Hodgson : J.T.L. Bone
S F. Hebeler   W. R. Nixon   D. N. P. Asher
Played 3 : Lost 2 : Drawn 1 :

Football Team.
1960.

constructed around Reading and part of the route was through the playing fields
of Frilsham House School - this school was therefore looking for somewhere else
to go. The school moved down to Watts House and was renamed Connaught and
Frilsham House School, the headmaster of Frilsham becoming the head of the
combined school. It was not a success, however, and the school had closed by 1968.
From this point Watts House went into rapid decline. The valve in the main water
tank, which was situated right up in the attic, above the dining room, got stuck,
and one day Wilfred Ford, who was acting as caretaker, opened the front door to
find water pouring out. The water had come from the tank through the old staff
bedrooms, all down the main staircase and out the front door.

Cedar Falls

It was another four years before the present owner, Mr Ray Smith, bought the
House.
Ray Smith as a teenager was a member of the Bedminster Boxing Club. He vividly
recalls talking to other boxers about the poor state of equipment in the club,

despite it being one of the best in the country. It was frequently mentioned that it would be splendid to have a top gymnasium with all the proper facilities. This became Ray's dream, to build a first class gym of his own.

After being demobbed from the Physical Training Corps of the Gloucester Regiment, two events changed the direction of Ray's life. He had taken up Judo through which he sustained a broken leg and prior to that he had a house fire. Believing that this patch of bad luck was some kind of omen, he said to his wife, "I've had enough of this, I'm going to be a builder."

At that time he had a plastering business with his father, so he sold the car, bought a plot of land and, at the age of 21, started the Ray Smith Group.

Over the following years he built up the business, joined, started or acquired other businesses, until there were nine altogether, as diverse as central heating, plant hire, builders merchants and a suede factory.

In 1972 one of the companies purchased Watts House, by auction, for its' development potential. In the years that followed there was an uphill battle with the planners.

One day Ray was coming up the drive in his car and he experienced a remarkable feeling of peace and tranquillity, which he attributes to the fact that a strong ley-line runs up the estate, through the Cedar Tree. He decided to make the house into a Health Farm with a golf course in the grounds, and a small development of flats beside the house. With a change in planning policy and attitudes, permission was given for the Health Farm, and building started 1981. It was finally to be the realisation of that boyhood dream.

Unfortunately it was nine years since the auction and in this time the lead had been stolen from the roof, as well as many of the fixtures and fittings, fireplaces and stone urns. Deterioration of the building had been rapid, with water coming in, and there was a lot of rotten wood and plasterwork.

The restoration of the house and grounds was a Smith Family enterprise. The work was directed by Ray and his two sons, Richard and Stephen, using many local firms and tradespeople. They were amazed at the quality of work, which was equal or better than the original, and several of these firms are still doing jobs at Cedar Falls. In August 1982, Watts House started a new life as Cedar Falls Health Farm. During this period the golf course was also constructed, the flats built and the grounds landscaped. Ray's daughter, Debbie, who had trained as a therapist in Bath, joined the staff in order to gain experience, and subsequently started two Health and Beauty Salons in Bristol. Many local people were employed and some have been at Cedar Falls for a long time. Several now hold senior positions.

During the renovation work an elderly lady came up to the house and insisted that her 'birthday tree' was not felled. This lady was Violet Bucknall (Boles). Tree planting had been a tradition in the Boles family to celebrate notable events. The tree was not removed and, in fact, the tradition of planting trees of commemoration has continued.

Renovation Work. 1981.
The main staircase before and after,

The Dining - rooms before restoration and in the insets the dining-rooms afterwards

The design of the golf course was conceived by Ray and his solicitor, Tony Elliott. This was achieved by them taking their golf clubs around the grounds and at strategic points striking a golf ball and where the ball alighted, they marked the position for the green. Tony was a very close friend and when he died, in his will, he stated that Ray could do whatever he wished with his ashes. For some time the urn graced the mantelpiece in the flat/office at Cedar Falls, and on several occasions it presided on the table at celebratory dinners. Eventually Ray decided to sprinkle the ashes on the greens of the golf course, apart from the 4th green - he decided that Tony would not be able to influence his putting on one green at least! There were still some ashes remaining (surprising for a man who was only around $9^1/_2$ stone), so a cedar tree was planted and the urn placed beneath it.

Guy Mitchell photographed in 1990 on the veranda of the men's changing room. The caption reads: ' Guy's Room - you can sing here as much as you like.' Guy, in fact, wrote a song wrote especially for Cedar Falls while on this trip.

Guy had always endeavoured to beat Ray Smith on the golf course and finally succeeded. He was a good artist and commemorated the event by drawing the picture shown left.

Several more of Ray's friends have had a tree planted in their memory, within the grounds at Cedar Falls.

One was the American singer Guy ('Singing the Blues') Mitchell. Ray was a great fan and eventually he managed to invite him down to Cedar Falls for a round of golf. They became very good friends and Guy made several visits when he was on tour in this country. When Guy died on 1st July 1999, Ray made a 'time capsule' of Guy Mitchell tapes and golfing equipment. This was placed beneath a newly planted tree. To this day the Guy Mitchell Golf Society Event is held annually at Cedar Falls.

Cedar Falls continues to be one of the most successful Health Farms in the country. Over the last twenty years, it has been visited by Royalty and many well-known personalities who have enjoyed the peace and tranquillity of the luxurious surroundings and still continue to do so.

Barbara Windsor, one of the many personalities who have stayed at Cedar Falls, opening the main dining-room.

The Asylum c 1911

— Six —
Cotford

Cotford Asylum

The Medical Superintendents

Cotford Memories

Cotford Asylum

Cotford nestles in one of the most secluded and picturesque spots in the Vale of Taunton Deane. As is well known to most of the residents in the surrounding locality, the wide bed of this fertile valley is by no means a flat and level stretch of country; it is broken up by numerous little eminences, which in shape closely resembles an inverted saucer, and which although they assume considerable importance in consequence of the low-lying nature of the surrounding country are yet insignificant molehills when compared with the frowning and majestic Blackdown and Cothelstone Hills. It is on the southern slope of one of these "mounds" that Cotford Farm commands extensive views of both ranges of hills, with the Wellington Monument as a prominent feature in one direction and the beacon tower on Cothelstone Hill another.

Cotford can scarcely be called a village or a hamlet, it might almost be said to be out of the beaten track altogether. From a peaceful and quietude point of view the site is well suited as an asylum for the insane.

The erection of the new asylum at Cotford, which has been in progress during the past four years, is now rapidly drawing to a completion, and a palatial and withall useful pile of buildings now present themselves to public view. At the foot of the building a babbling brooklet meanders under a canopy of alders, and it is probably from this little brook that the homestead, Cotford Farm, derives its name.

The Somerset County Herald - Saturday 5th June 1897.

The building was designed by Giles Gough and Trollope, who won a competition for the design in 1891. The Secretary of State gave approval for the building in 1892, which was to cost £113,300. The Asylum opened in 1897.

The Asylum was built as a series of pavilions around a central service core, linked by a corridor of a flattened U-plan. On either side of a central administration block were four separate pavilions for four distinct classes of patient, connected by a corridor, the male wards on the east (right of the entrance to the clock tower) and female to the west. The large hall and kitchen occupied the heart of the complex, and the laundry and workshops were behind. There was a separate isolation wing, farm and a number of staff houses (The Villas). The farm once occupied the Dene Barton site.

The tradition of continuous family employment has all but disappeared from the structure of British life. However, over nearly a hundred years, a large family spirit built up at Cotford. Indeed there was a great deal of inter-marriages so that it became difficult to know who was related to another member of staff. The fact that several generations of families found secure employment at Cotford was a factor in the growth and composition of the village of Bishops Lydeard.

FIRST ARRIVALS - A LUNATIC AT LARGE - EXCITING CHASE

Our Norton Fitzwarren Correspondent writes:

The first contingent of Lunatics from Wells Asylum, numbering about 50 male and female, passed through this village on Saturday afternoon last on their way to the new asylum at Cotford. The whole journey from Wells was covered by road, the patients being conveyed in four large open brakes each of which was in the charge of wardens and attendants.

No incident occurred to mar the journey until the strangers had almost reached their destination when one of the male patients suddenly leaped over the side of the brake and bolted down the road at a very rapid pace. A couple of attendants started off in pursuit and ultimately succeeded in attracting the attention of a man engaged in cracking stones by the roadside, and this worthy courageously brought the runaway to bay when he was promptly secured and quietly marched back to the seat he had so recently vacated. Needless to say the incident, which was quite close to the village, created considerable excitement among the residents.

Somerset County Herald 29th May 1897.

The numbers of patients soon swelled and at their height reached 1200. There were 24 ancillary staff and the patients were looked after by 37 nurses known as 'attendants', who wore prison guard style uniforms, with a chain round their waist carrying keys and a whistle. All doors were kept locked. Admissions of voluntary patients were rare until after the Second World War and the majority of patients were subject to compulsory detention under the then Lunacy Acts. It was not unknown for patients to be admitted tied up with ropes because of violent behaviour. There were four padded rooms on each side of the hospital and the most commonly used sedatives were bromides administered by the two Medical Officers two or three times a week.

A male nurse caught talking to a female employee could be instantly dismissed and anyone reporting late three times in a month could also lose his or her job. This was highlighted in a 1902 report: "*we would also point out that three men working in the laundry are in association with the women. It is within our knowledge that the practice has elsewhere resulted in serious consequences and we trust, therefore, that in this asylum it will be discontinued.*"

The Asylum became known as Tone Vale Hospital in 1945 but it was not until the 1950's that the sixteen-feet high railings were removed from around the hospital. It was only at this time that the community were more willing to accept psychiatric patients.

The 290-acre site was a self-contained community with its own water supply, sewage works and burial ground. It had a market garden, a laundry, cobblers, upholsterers, bakers, butchers, a large herd of Friesian cows and a farm with 6,000 poultry to supply eggs and meat to the hospital. Patients were encouraged to work receiving tokens, which could be exchanged for sweets or cigarettes.

A 1d Token which could be exchanged for sweets, cigarettes etc.

From the early days a cricket field and football pitch existed and facilities for rugby, bowls, putting and netball were added, along with an art therapy centre and pet farm. As well as outstanding sports facilities the Hospital had its own ballroom, cinema and, at one stage, even its own dance band.

St Lukes Chapel

A Male Ward

The Gardens

The map below shows the site and layout of
Cotford Mental Hospital
(the Chapel and main block still exist)

Ballroom c. 1930

Water Tower

Cotford Farm

The Medical Superintendents

Dr. Henry Aveline

The regime at Cotford Asylum was very rigid and the Medical Superintendent was very much in charge and made all the final decisions.

Dr Henry Aveline was the first Medical Superintendent at Cotford and he was a very colourful and interesting character. He came to Cotford from Bristol Asylum and it is thought that he trained in London and spent some time at the famous Bethlem Hospital (Bedlam). His father had been the Somerset County Geologist and worked with Sir Thomas de la Beche on the local part of the first National Geological Survey of Britain. When he first came to Cotford he was single, but married in 1904 - his wife came from the Totnes area - and they had three daughters.

Henry spoke ten languages and was fluent in Esparanto, in fact he was one of the promoters for the use of Esparanto. He was widely travelled and his hobbies included art, pressed flowers, collecting birds eggs and was keen on nature in general. In addition bookbinding was another of his interests. He was the proud owner of a 'Genevieve' type car - a Darique and was one of the first members of the Automobile Association in Somereset. The tale was told of him having to drive the car backwards up Porlock Hill with his wife and daughters walking up, hoping he would make it to the top without incident! During the First World War the car had to be given up for a time and the family used a governess cart instead. The chauffeur, Mr Gay, became the groom. The horse had a habit of becoming frisky and jumping the puddles which always formed at Cross Keys, on the journey to Taunton. Dr Aveline and his family lived in Cotford House now Orchard Lodge, which had been built for the Superintendents of the Asylum.

Dr W.S. Graham, who had been at Cotford since 1907 as Deputy Superintendent, succeeded Dr Aveline as Superintendent. He was a batchelor and lived in Cotford House with his sister, Miss Graham, as his housekeeper. Dr Graham had two

Cotford House 1918.
Hettie and Anette
Aveline

Medical Officers and the medical routine was that they were to await Dr Graham's arrival, outside his office, each day at 10 a.m. There were no written reports in those days, the Medical Officers reported verbally to the Superintendent any incidents which had occurred affecting the patients in their charge and he questioned them and discussed appropriate action. Dr Graham took any necessary executive action, such as reports of patient death, all of which had to be reported to the coroner. The Medical Officers then did the rounds of all the wards accompanied by the Matron or Head Male Nurse.

Dr F.J. Manning joined the staff on 4th August 1937 and he was a Medical Officer, living in a hospital flat and was paid £550 per annum. He recalled:

Before the Second World War there were four padded rooms on each side of the hospital and the most commonly used sedatives were paraldehyde and bromides which were most effective until superseded by more modern equivalents. There was no dispenser on the staff, the other Medical Officer, Dr Healy, and myself were responsible for the issue of drugs which we undertook some two or three times a week. The regime was very authoritarian and annual visits were made to all mental institutions by the Commissioners of the Board of Control. These visits were unannounced although occasionally a 'tip off' was received from another hospital that they were in the vicinity. Their visits were very detailed and Cotford was always concerned that it be shown in a favourable light. I remember an occasion when Dr Graham and I were just leaving for a day at the races when the Commissioners suddenly appeared in the drive. That was the end of our race day and we had turn back to the hospital. Dr Graham was not amused and his displeasure took days to dispel!

I recall one incident when one of the male patients escaped one night from a padded room in which he was being confined. He made his way to Dene Court, which at that time was occupied by a lady who kept horses in the stables. He broke in and took one of the horses. Barebacked and wearing just a blanket he rode into Bishops Lydeard. By this time the alarm had been raised and he was apprehended there saying, " Jesus rode into Jerusalem on an ass and I'm going to ride into Minehead on a horse."

Dr Kenneth Bailey became Superintendent of Cotford in October 1945. It was still a 'mental asylum' complete with iron railings, a prison-like system of locked doors, padded rooms and a cupboard full of straight-jackets. He was a stockily built, forthright man, whose pugnacious ardour was tempered with a bubbling good humour. Prejudice lingered on for years, a natural prejudice born of fear and misunderstanding - "Cotford" was used in a derogatory way or as a term of abuse - despite the change of name to Tone Vale Hospital.

Dr Bailey had the railings removed and the doors opened, through which an increasing stream of friends and visitors came to mingle with the patients. The fear gradually subsided.

Right: Dr Bailey and Miss Needham, Matron (seated), with Student Nurse Ruth Thompson.

The Medical Health Act of 1957 abolished the post of Medical Superintendent and Dr Bailey became a Consultant together with four others, one of whom was Dr Manning, each with the title 'Responsible Medical Officer'. More were appointed from 1974 onwards.

Below: Dr Graham and Miss Nichol, Matron, with the female nurses of the time.

Cotford Memories

Mrs Minnie Eller. At the age of eighteen, Minnie went to Cotford in 1924 having been educated in Bridgend. Her sister Enid Chappell, twenty years her senior, was already a nurse there and completed 34 years service.

My sister was trained as a tailoress and made our uniforms. As a newcomer I was given one of the four beds under the Clock Tower. After three years I took a written exam and an oral exam, conducted by Dr Aveline and an outside Doctor. Two years later I qualified as a nurse and was promoted to a Ward Sister. My pay rose from £3 a month when I started to £8. The hours were long and very often, if someone was absent, we had to work two shifts in succession, 6.30 a.m. to 2.30 a.m. the following morning. Trade Unions had just been formed and we had to meet by the bridge over the little stream to discuss our working conditions.

Staff usually had one day off in the week and we used to cycle to friends houses in Bishop's Lydeard or to dances in the village halls of Cothelstone, Oake or Staplegrove. One of my best friends, a nurse, was the daughter of Mr Burgess, the butler at Watts House. On Saturday nights there would be a filmshow or a dance in the ballroom when male patients were allowed to dance with female patients. There were other entertainments. I remember a group called the Tantums - Carlos Tantum was a harpist and he performed with his Mum and Dad. Each Christmas there was a pantomime put on by the staff, with some patients doing stage management. The Christmas Ball was attended by the gentry, in their black tie evening suits and ball gowns. Squire Esdaile always came.

I became very fond of some patients. Mrs Julia Wright, the ex-postmistress from Bishops Lydeard, frequently came into the nurse's kitchen and on one occasion she was helping me cook a rabbit that had been caught by the Canadian male nurses. Cooking with patients was not really permitted and it coincided with a surprise visit by Dr Aveline.

"Cooking I presume," he said.

"Yes, sir," I replied.

"By the smell you are obviously not cooking dressings!"

"No, sir"

Although very strict keeping things up to scratch, the Superintendent was also very caring. I once had terrible tonsillitis and Dr Graham came down in the middle of the night and immediately lanced my tonsils.

Some patients took it upon themselves to look after me. Miss Massey (from the famous acting family) looked after my room but also had no hesitation in reading my 'love letters' from my future husband! Another patient, Mrs Coward, who had six or seven children and whose husband was cowherd on Cotford Farm, took it upon herself to guard my bedroom. "What's yours is mine," she used to say. When I became a Ward Sister one was officially allowed to choose a patient to act as a 'maid'. My maid was Rachael Clarke.

Mrs Wearmouth and Mrs Eller dressed for their parts in the Pantomime c.1925.

Mrs Wearmouth. In 1919, at the home of her grandparents in Lower Cottages (South Villas), Mrs Wearmouth was born. Like many families of the time they worked at the Asylum. Her grandfather was a Master Carpenter who worked on the ballroom with its fine wooden panelled walls, doors and ceiling (the latter covered up in the 1950's to create the cinema facilities). Her father was a clerk in the Clerk of Works Office and her uncle was a butcher at Cotford.

It must be remembered that the Asylum was a totally self-sufficient community, hence the need for a butcher and all other trades. The patients worked on the farm and in the grounds. Cattle and pigs were kept and a firm in Taunton regularly supplied pig swill to help feed the pigs. Chicken were kept in an area near the nurses home. As the produce from the farm and grounds was only for the patients and not for the staff families, all necessities were delivered to Cotford residents.

Growing up, for a child living on the Asylum complex, was no problem. As a youngster I was able to go to the Saturday dances held in the large hall. I can recall dancing with the patients - male patients sat on one side of the hall and female patients on the other. The music was provided by an organ, the music being generated from perforated rolls. Concerts were given by the Wellington Band and later by the Taunton Concert Band. Friday night was usually the cinema night.

As a child I remember Dr Aveline who adhered strictly to the rules and his Matron, Miss Miller. Later came Miss Nichol and Miss Needham. On duty in the main entrance was a Hall Boy, in a smart uniform, complete with shiny buttons and a hat, to help and direct callers.

The Christmas Ball in the early 1950's

BACK ROW
S.Rugg F.Lindford J.Stone J.Tacchie G.Gosney
F.Tizzard (V. Pres.)

MIDDLE ROW
C.Chard K.Shutter F.Lindford E.Williams J.Reed
A.Sully (Sec.)
R.Gosney L.Anning M.Barter (Treas.)

FRONT ROW
C.Brice F.Northey Dr. Mackay Dr.Graham Dr.
Manning (V. Capt.) (V. Pres.) (Pres.) (V. Pres.)

J.Marsden J.Dury (Capt.)

Each year a pantomime or plays were put on by the staff and volunteers in the Hospital.

Above left shows the pantomime of 1915 and right a play during the Second World War.

Left The Tone Vale Players c.1951.

Mr Jim Stutt. Jim started work at Cotford in 1931 as a young electrical engineer and worked his way up to become the Building Manager. He completed 40 years service there. His father had worked on the building when the Asylum was being constructed in the 1890's and he wryly stated that - 'what the father built, the son destroyed.'

Part of my work involved putting into practice many of the changes that were necessary to move from the concept of a Lunatic Asylum to a Hospital, following the inception of the NHS, on 'the appointed day' in July 1948. The Asylum was reborn as Tone Vale Hospital.

When my father worked on the building much of the sandstone was quarried at Bishops Lydeard but some bricks were kilned on site, using the clay that was extracted when the site was prepared. They were moulded to a special size (9" x 4" x 3¹/₂").
Many of the original moulding tools and carpenter's tools were kept for years until the disposal sale in 1994. In conjunction with the Chairman, John Hope, I turned, with direct labour, the Hospital inside out. The railings were removed which had been a feature of the Asylum and enclosed the site. The best of these railings were then taken to form a screen in the Chapel. The wards were changed so that they could look out on the newly landscaped gardens. Dr Hungerford, a Management Committee member and keen bowls player, was able to obtain the replaced bowls pavilion from Vivary Park, which the patients then transformed into an excellent centre for cricket and bowls. Before being a pavilion at Vivary Park it had previously served as a cabby's kiosk on the Parade in Taunton.

I had two other duties at the Hospital. The first was to act as Undertaker and when the Cotford burial ground was full, burials took place at Bishops Lydeard churchyard. Secondly I was leader of the Fire Brigade.

The Hospital generated its own electricity. The picture shows the electrical installation, run by Mr Grimstone, in 1931.

Mr George Grimstone. George came from Stockport, serving with the Royal Engineers in the Great War and was one time stationed at Sandhill Park. He met and married Florence Hepzibah Clarke, the daughter of the Postmaster of Bishops Lydeard. At the time of his death in 1965, aged 74, he was Superintendent Engineer at the Hospital.

During my years at Tone Vale I carried out a number of improvements to the electrical services at the Hospital, including the installation of a new automatic telephone exchange. Most of the old equipment found its way to Ballifants Farm where my nephew, the young Arthur C. Clarke, took everything apart to see how it worked, and then built his own system. This experience gave Arthur an interest in communications, and later led to his research preceding the foundation of the communications satellite network and the origin of the "Clarke Orbit".

Mr Douglas Wade. Douglas was trained as a Registered Mental Nurse at Tone Vale Hospital following an earlier career with the Gas Board.

A few years after Dr Bailey's arrival the drug Largactil became available which transformed the way patients were treated. With the subsequent introduction of tranquillisers, the way was open for Dr Bailey to introduce the unlocked wards. By 1963 the practice of insulin therapy for schizophrenics ended. It had been customary treatment to use insulin (as for diabetics) in a very large dose to produce a calming effect. Leucotomy operations were still carried out in the early years of Tone Vale, but they had a limited success rate and were abandoned as progress with treatments advanced.

The daily work routine started with most of the patients setting off each morning to do work in the many units of self-sufficiency - the farm (including the pig and poultry unit), concrete block making, the bakery, carpentry, laundry, gardening which included greenhouse propagation. There was a wrought iron workshop where Harry Horobin, the well-known west country metalworker, worked and taught patients his skills. These occupations gave shape and meaning to the everyday lives of the patients and assisted in their recovery process. On-site dental and chiropody services were provided, and of course cooking and shopping skills, so essential to those who had been away from normal life for a considerable time. This led eventually towards patients leaving the Hospital to live in small home-style communities, the start of 'Care in the Community'.

No memories are complete without a story of animals. The Tone Vale cats were notorious- there were so many feral cats roaming the Hospital and grounds that the RSPCA had to be called regularly to deal with them. Rats and cockroaches were in abundance on which they fed. Maybe the picture was not so rosy in the past as some people remember!

Mr Ernest Stephens. Ernest was appointed Head Gardener at Tone Vale in 1958. As the idea of containment gave way to landscaping and patient involvement, many patients who had vegetated in long-stay wards for years saw a new life emerge under his sympathetic care.

The purchase of greenhouses at a knock-down price, when Napiers (carnation growers) of Taunton closed down in 1962, enabled me to develop the grounds in an adventurous way, landscaping the front of the Hospital around a water wheel from Cotford Farm and installing a mist propagator in the greenhouses at the rear of the Hospital. The trees, plants and shrubs became available for hospitals throughout the region. Gold medals were won for four successive years at the Taunton Flower Show.

Mr William 'Bill' Hares. Bill worked at Tone Vale from the early 1950's and was Catering Manager and the branch secretary of Confederation Of Health Service Employees. The branch of the National Asylum Workers Union at Cotford was formed in 1910 and, as recalled by Mrs Minnie Eller, had to meet secretly on the old river bridge. It was not until January 1946 when Dr Bailey addressed the Branch Meeting saying, "It has taken a war to bring people together in a common purpose, and I sincerely hope the same spirit will prevail in the days of peace," that the union and management began working as a team and were equal in the contributions to the everyday running of the Hospital.

The task of the catering staff was difficult at the best, cost cutting and the two World Wars adding to the burden of trying to feed a thousand plus patients and some two hundred staff, but feed them they did. The cooks, just after the Second War, were 'Pop' Lovell, Arthur Smith, Bert Burland and Cliff Creed, to name but a few. They provided good wholesome food, but some of the menus read 'Cornflakes with Milk' and, on one day 'bread with margarine', then every other day, 'bread with butter'. 'Tripe and Onions' and 'Chitterlings' (the cooked small intestines of a pig) were regular weekly features on the patients' menu.

Meat and eggs came from our farm and all the vegetables from the gardens, which meant that when a particular vegetable was abundant it was supplied until it ran out. It was little wonder that when carrots were in season everyone in the Hospital walked around with an 'orange glow' and could see very well in the dark!

These were the days of the 'stock pot'. Tone Vale kitchen had an enormous one bubbling away on the centre stove, looking like something out of "Quatermass" and smelling even worse. I remember an outbreak of salmonella on one of the male wards. The stock pot was the first thing to be investigated, although this was found not to be the cause.

On a lighter vein, every kitchen has its own comedian. Cliff Creed, the staff cook, was Tone Vales'. I remember being in the kitchen one Monday morning when a new recruit arrived, a kitchen porter. Cliff went to great lengths and in somewhat gory detail to explain the function of the Hospital and what kind of patients worked in the kitchen, putting the fear of the devil into the poor chap. At the end of the pep talk he

Above: The old and new Kitchen of the Hospital. Mr Sedgbeer is in the picture on the right.

Left: Bill Hares (left), with the cook, looking at the poultry for the menu

told the new porter that he would be working with one of the patients in the wash-up. If the patient started saying he could see "little green men" walking around then the porter was told to say that he could see them as well. For an hour or so the two worked in absolute silence washing up the greasy pots. Then, not being able to stand the silence any longer, the new kitchen porter said, "Look there, can you see those little green men under the sink? They have jumped up now on to the top." In one movement the old patient, who had not said a word, grabbed his coat and was out through the door, saying to Cliff Creed on his way out, "I'm off back to the ward. I'm not working out there with him. He's nuts - seeing little green men jumping all over the place!"

In 1979 I had need to look for a house to accommodate my young son and myself. The North Lodge had become run down since its last occupants Jim Gay and his wife had retired. Jim's father had been the chauffeur to Dr Aveline and Jim had carried on from his father to become chief mechanic. The Gay family had been the only family to occupy the Lodge. The Lodge was upgraded and I moved in with my son.

It was in the first week that I woke in the early hours of the morning, to see a little old lady standing near the wardrobe. Thinking one of the female residents had somehow been able to get out of the Hospital and I had forgotten to lock the back door, I said, getting out of bed, "How on earth have you managed to get in here?" As I went towards her she turned and walked through the wardrobe, slowly disappearing. The hairs on the back of my neck stood up. My immediate reaction was to check my son, David, was alright in the next room. He was fast asleep.

The following morning, in conversation with Eric Drake, the surgical shoemaker for the Hospital, I told him of what I could only believe was a bad dream. He looked at me in amazement when I described the old lady. He said, "Well dream or not, you have just described in detail old Mrs Gay, Jim's mother. That's exactly the way she dressed." I had never met her.

The same afternoon I was approached by the Hospital physiotherapist, Mrs Wilde. She said, "I hear from Mr Drake you've experienced a visitation. Don't worry she only came to see who was living in her house. You'll never see her again."

Mrs Wilde was right, even though I was afraid to put the light out for two weeks, she never did come back.

On the 5th April 1995 a final Thanksgiving Service was held in the Chapel of St Luke, Tone Vale at which the Bishop of Bath and Wells preached. Over the previous ten years patients had been gradually moved into ready-built accommodation in the local communities. Tone Vale Hospital finally closed.

The Health Authority marketed the site for development as a 600-home village to include shops, play areas and a Primary School. Buildings such as the core of the main Hospital, the Chapel, the Superintendent's House and two Lodges were to be retained.

Many readers will identify fondly with the street names of Cotford St Luke : Aveline Court, Graham Way, Baileys Gate, Manning Drive, Nichol Place, Healeys Meadow and Needhams Patch.

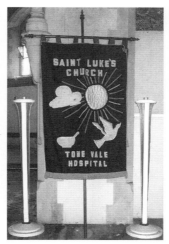

Top: The railings in the side chapel were made from those which enclosed the Hospital.
Bottom: The decoration on the wall of the chancel

Top: St Lukes is unique in having separate entrance doors for male and female patients.
Bottom: The vandalised organ.

Left: The outside staircase used by the Medical Superintendent and his family which led to (right) the box inside the church.
Above: The mosiac on the side of the Superintendent's box

The village of Bishops Lydeard looking north

— Seven —
Tales from the Twentieth Century

The village of Bishops Lydeard looking south

Tales from the Twentieth Century

This chapter, in the history of the village, has been compiled using the minutes of the Parish Council and Parish Meetings interspersed with the recollections of people who lived here during the last century. An interesting picture is revealed of how the inhabitants coped with two World Wars and the way the social and environmental conditions of their lives improved.

By 1897, the year of Queen Victoria's Diamond Jubilee, Britain dominated the world through its industrial achievement in a century of dramatic change. The countryside had also been the setting for radical change, as the landscape was dramatically altered by the property enclosures of rural landlords and the agricultural revolution. Ironically, this rural revolution which included the creation of our present field system with its hedgerows and clumps of trees, has become regarded as a precious part of our landscape heritage.

Thirteen years prior to the Jubilee, the Third Reform Act had ended aristocratic government by extending the franchise to the working classes - the first time that the vote was disassociated from some kind of property qualification. By 1900 it did not make economic sense to establish a rural power base since landowning had ceased to be a passport to power. With the departure of the Lethbridge family, the new generation of landed estate owners, like Dennis Boles, was living according to a new cultural ideal, where the English Country Squire, whose pursuit of leisure, commitment to political service and cultivation of style, set the highest standards within the framework provided by the country house.

Charles Esdaile, first Chairman of Bishops Lydeard Parish Council

The Local Government Act of 1894 gave rise to the formation of a Parish Council for a rural parish, to be elected from among the parochial electors of that parish. On 4th December 1894 a Parish Meeting was held in the schoolroom of Bishops Lydeard, Mr. George Saunders taking the chair at 6:55pm, when 17 nomination papers were handed in for the six seats of the new Parish Council. The Chairman carefully examined the papers and waited until 7:30pm. When no further nominations were forthcoming the candidates were read out to the meeting. Mr. Saunders then asked for a show of hands in favour of each candidate, taken in alphabetical order. This was duly completed. However Dr. Fligg, Dr. Frossard and Mr. Hunt demanded a Poll be called. The Poll took place on 15th December 1894 in the schoolroom from 12 noon to 2pm and 4pm to 8pm. The results were announced by George Saunders the same evening. The following gentlemen were declared elected to serve as councillors on the Bishops Lydeard Parish Council:

Walter Darby [Miller] 139, Charles Esdaile Esq. [Cothelstone] 114, William Sweeting [Baker] 102, Walter Hanks [Jobmaster]

112, Walter Lickfold [Butcher] and Frederick Martin [Grocer] 88.
The first meeting of the Council took place in the schoolroom on 31st December 1894 at 10:30am when Charles Esdaile was elected Chairman, and Walter Darby Vice Chairman. The people of Bishops Lydeard were now able to have a democratic voice in shaping the conditions in which they lived. Their concerns over the next century centred around housing, traffic, lighting, litter in the village, flooding and the lengthy time bureaucracy took to get things done. The same issues still concern us today at the start of the 21st century!

On the Move

In the early years of the century footpaths were always a constant concern. There were few cars so most had to walk. There was great inconvenience to inhabitants from distant parts of the Parish to get to the village due to the state of the paths, particularly from the Gore Inn [Lethbridge Arms] to Tithill and from Watts Bridge to Ash Priors. What traffic there was through the village caused notices to be attached to the lamp posts, in September 1907, requesting motorists to go slowly through the village. Sam Doble [Carpenter] had been paid 3/6d for fixing the noticeboards but they were removed in February 1911. By 1922 attention was being drawn to the dangerous crossway at Gore Square and that warning notices should be placed there. The road past The Lethbridge was the main road from Taunton to Minehead at that time. Three years later the attention of the Ministry of Transport was drawn to this matter, with the request that caution notices might be erected. At the same time Capt. Parkman [Bell Inn] said he had received various complaints about the heavy traffic caused by Mr. King's steam lorries continually coming up from Watts Bridge through the village. Mr. King was requested not to use the village for his lorries unless absolutely necessary.
On 24th March 1948 an accident occurred in Gore Square at 9:30pm. Mrs. Percival reported difficulty in getting a policeman to the scene of the accident. No policeman was available from the village and it was an hour and a quarter before the police from Taunton arrived!
The village was considering the idea of traffic lights at Gore Square by March 1958, as being the cheapest and most effective way of resolving the traffic problem. Somerset County Council seemed to take this idea seriously. Two years later traffic lights were turned down by the Ministry of Transport, after a road census, and the subject of a by-pass was discussed. The village, however, was not in favour of its construction saying:
We oppose the by-pass on the grounds that:
1. The cost would be excessive.
2. It would bring a speed-free road increasing the danger to inhabitants of Sandhill, Greenway and Lynchfield when crossing.
3. It would destroy too much valuable agricultural land without overcoming the

danger at Gore Square.

Edward Du Cann M.P. was drawn into the argument as both the Rural District Council and the Parish Council supported traffic lights. The Minister refused to change his mind in 1961 so the RDC withdrew its objection. Somerset County Council said they would build a subway beneath the new road. On this condition the Parish Council agreed to the by-pass being built.

In 1964 Mrs. Hill was urging that pressure should be made to get the road works started. The by-pass was finally completed in 1967.

Gladys Palmer. *When I was a young girl we used the train to go to Taunton. Each week I went with my friend to Taunton Arts College in Corporation Street. We walked to the station and it cost 8d return to Taunton. We paid 1/- for the drawing lesson and that left 4d from the 2/- we had each week, so we went to Moor's Restaurant at the corner of St James Street and had a cup of tea and a pork pie.*

Walter Hanks operated the only other means of transport. He had a horse-drawn brake, with no cover, which had five seats each side and you entered up steps at the back. You could nearly walk as quickly to Taunton in the time it took the horse! Very often at Penn Elm the horse got tired and the passengers would have to get out and walk up the hill. Percy, Walter's son, was in the First War and while he was abroad he had won the Calcutta sweepstake. With the winnings he returned and bought the first mechanical bus. This was like a little workman's lorry, it had a canvas cover and you entered up the steps on the back where Walter would stand to collect the money. Later Walter and Percy bought the first real bus - bright red. The other buses at that time were the Lavender Blue from Minehead, Withers from Bagborough, Western National and Dunn's Motors from Taunton. Western National eventually bought them all out.

Walter was also the 'transportation of the dead'. He used to take the bier up to the Church. In the same shed was an old Bath chair for the 'transportation of the disabled'. [The door to this shed still exists off Mount Street, before A.J. Raucki's Yard].

Let there be light!

The lighting of streets is something we take for granted nowadays. In 1895 the Parish Council took over the responsibility of lighting the village, the oil for which would cost £20 that year. A lamplighter, John Mullins, was appointed on eight shillings a week to light the lamps during the winter season.

In 1904 John Mullins resigned through ill health and Harry Shattock was appointed to commence his duties in September.

The following guidelines were drawn up:

1. The Lamplighter shall keep the lanterns clean and the wicks well trimmed.

2. Lamps to be lit each evening during the lighting season from one hour after sunset until 10:15pm except as per rule 3.

3. No lamps need to be lit after the moon is seven days old until two days after

full, unless the sky is overcast with clouds and light is required.

4. In case of repairs the Lamplighter shall consult the Lighting Directors [two appointed members of the Parish Council].

5. Wages to be paid weekly as per contract.

6. The Fire Brigade Station to be used for storage etc., the Lamplighter to be furnished with a key.

By March 1915 it was reported that Mr. Shattock had refused to start the street lighting. Mr. Charles Bond was appointed, but by the September said he would not to carry out the duties unless he was paid ten shillings - a week. The Parish Council did not feel justified to pay this increase and abandoned lighting for that season. The streets of Bishops Lydeard, in fact, remained in darkness for the remainder of the First World War and lighting only resumed in the winter of 1919 when Mr. Hughes became the Lamplighter.

Above. An engraving of a Lamplighter taken from the Parish Magazine of the time.

Below. The light outside George Axe's shop. He subscribed to electricity in 1927.
The steps beyond his shop, up to the almshouses, were known as 'The Cassey Steps.'

In September 1921 the village was asked who would want electricity if it were brought to the village, by extending the main from Staplegrove. The cost would be £1500 and would be paid for by those who had the electricity. In 1924 Somerset County Council, however, agreed to provide a cable from Taunton to Sandhill and in the following year Taunton Town Council agreed to provide electricity for lighting, providing the Parish Council paid for the electricity and maintained the lamps. The Parish Council would also have to pay £150 towards installation costs.

At a meeting in December 1925 it was stated that 35 signatures would be needed to subscribe to electricity to their homes in order to repay the £150 to the Council. Each subscriber was to pay ten shillings a quarter for two years. At that meeting 26 names were taken and Commander Elliot offered to canvass the village for the rest. By February 1927 Commander Elliot reported that at last the scheme had been approved by the Electricity Commission and Taunton Town Council. In July of that year a ten year agreement was made with the Taunton Electricity Department for 22 electric lamps. On the evening of 13th February 1928 the Chairman of the Council, Mr. Lampson, proceeded to Gore Square together with members of the Council and switched on the lights. For the first time street lighting would be provided in the summer months as well as winter, if required.

Home Sweet Home

Gladys Palmer. *In 1914 George Hartnell built a new house, with four bedrooms, at the top end of the village. My father rented it and called it Roseneath because he had built an archway of roses. Later in the War we moved to Surgery House [now called Birch House, Church Street]. Mother looked after the surgery, which Dr. Frossard rented from Mrs. Pavey, and the Church Room. We lived behind the Church Room on the ground floor and stairs led up to the surgery and consulting room.*

There was a big cooking range, on a stone floor, and my mother, having just left a new house, often broke down and cried because she couldn't get it clean. We had no carpet down just coconut matting.

Dr. Frossard finished surgery around lunchtime. There were 23 doors in the rambling house and there were three little staircases down from our bedrooms. We used to open all the doors to play hide and seek throughout the afternoon.

Pat Lathbury. *My first attempt at acting took place in the dark back room, with its old cob wall, in which was a large old table. Gladys, the baker's daughter and I used to get up on the table using it as a stage. Once we got so animated, waving our arms about, that we knocked over the oil lamp, fortunately without serious consequences.*

Gladys continues. *The first Council Houses to be built were on the Minehead Road, Halfyard (Quantock View) was then built on the allotments. Houses were built on Garden Fields, as they were called, up over Cleeve Hill, in Pound Lane, and finally in Mill Lane. Baths were put into the houses at Halfyard. Hot water was heated in a 'copper' and the water was brought in buckets to fill the bath. Later gas was connected and gas geysers were fitted - they were deadly things. The geyser would be put on and often the pilot light would not light properly and when it did there would be a big explosion across the kitchen!*

Monday was wash day and there were other set days for ironing and the cleaning of rooms. If the wind was in the wrong direction the copper boiler wouldn't light and it would take ages to heat the water. It took all day to do the washing, then the clothes were put through the big mangle and hung out on the washing line.

Mary Bird. *I remember 'The Buildings' [now Delta Rise]. My aunt and uncle, Mr. and Mrs. Broom, lived there in one room with a huge picture of Queen Victoria on the wall. At the back there was a scullery and a staircase led up to three very small bedrooms. It always smelled musty and cockroaches were prevalent.*

Don Saunders. *I was born in 19 Church Street. This row of cottages was known as the 'New Buildings'. The whole block had to share three outside toilets down the garden path. There was just a tap outside, there was no sink inside. Baths were taken in a zinc bath in front of the fire on a Friday night. The water was carried outside the next morning and emptied down the sink.*

Dr. Philip Woodgate-Jones. *We lived in Warre Cottage [now Frog House]. It had been built on the stables of Warre House, by Mrs. Colthurst. The Miss Eves, who had* *been evacuated from Birmingham and bought Warre House, probably because it had a room big enough for their grand piano, moved back to Birmingham, so I bought Warre House. Having just connected Warre Cottage to the new main sewer, blow me down if I had to do the same for Warre House as everything from there went straight into the Mill Stream! The interesting thing is that there were many more trout in that stream with everything flowing into it, than afterwards. There was a thatched summerhouse in the garden with a loo at the back. This had a pipe from the stream through the loo and back down to the stream at the bottom!*

In September 1917 Taunton Rural District Council had asked if there would be sufficient housing in the Parish following the War. In June 1919 it was reported that, allowing for houses which could be repaired, 25 new houses would meet requirements.

Throughout the next decade a lot of pressure was exerted to improve the social conditions within the village in the way of housing, household waste, sewerage and water supplies. Complaints, for example, were made in April 1920 and again in 1923 by Mr. Creed with regard to the disgraceful state of the sewer in Frog Street outside his property, Rodney Cottage [now Captains Cottage], which was constantly overflowing and a danger to health. The streets were always in a dirty state and strewn with a waste paper.

Despite the building of some Council Houses, by 1925 it was still considered that there was a great shortage of workmen's dwellings, there being cases of overcrowding, while some occupied houses were not fit for habitation. The earth closets that had been put into the new houses in Pound Lane were considered unacceptable. The RDC refused to provide water closets draining into the surface water sewer, as they were of the opinion that a proper sewerage scheme should be provided and this would entail a very heavy expense on the Parish. They did, however, agree to provide covers for the closets and consider the question of providing better ventilation!

The following year the feeling in the village was very strong that the existing scheme of sewerage generally was inadequate and the time had come when health must take precedence over the rates. It was noted that the sewers were not being flushed as they were when first installed. Mr. Axe reported that great inconvenience was often caused to visitors in the village through there being no public lavatory and he wondered if the Police Authorities would allow the urinal adjoining the Police House to be open for public use.

By the end of the decade the dumping of household refuse was so bad that Sergeant Hiscox made an official complaint, the RDC replying that it was still awaiting instructions from the Ministry of Health. In March 1930 Mr.T. Penny gave permission to deposit the house refuse from the village in his brickyard at Bishops Hull. The W.I. was invited to arrange a scheme for collecting the rubbish.

This they did until October 1936 when Miss Gibson, on behalf of the W.I., felt that the time had come for the RDC to take over responsibility for the refuse. It did so in 1937.

By 1932 the new Halfyard Cottages had been completed followed by the cottages in Mill Lane, but the District Council was still not prepared to put in flush toilets until a new sewerage scheme had been installed. In 1937 a gravitational scheme was costed at £7500, 25% of the cost coming from the RDC and the rest to be found as a special rate on the Parish of 10 1/2d in the £ per year. The scheme was finally connected in 1941.

The Halfyard Cottages now called Quantock View

This did not immediately help the inhabitants of the Council houses, who had now been provided with buckets, for in March 1945 a petition was raised by all the residents of the houses in Pound Lane, Halfyard and Mill Lane, that they should no longer suffer the objectionable sanitary conditions and that flush lavatories should be installed in all council cottages in the Parish.

As late as 1949 the Public Health Officer was urged to speed up repairs and drainage to two cottages in Piffin Lane. There was a problem of cars parking in stagnant pools of water in the Lane due to the cottages being occupied by 11 persons using only one W.C.! The library now stands on the site of these cottages. Following the Second World War there was again a housing crisis. By 1952 the Darby Way Estate (named after Hubert Darby, late chairman of the Parish Council) was completed and Mr. Worrall M.P. reported that the temporary housing estate at Sandhill had to be cleared by 1956 and at that time there would be 160 people in need of rehousing. It was decided in 1955 to build a new estate in Greenway Wood, but the work on clearing the site took some two years and the estate was not completed until 1958.

The plans and layout for a new estate [Hither Mead] were first discussed in March 1966, however a scheme for the alleviation of the continuing flooding in Frog Street had to be resolved first. This was done in 1976 and the new estate was completed by 1981.

Another Water Debate.

From the Parish Meeting of 14th May 1921.

Mr. Dawe, Clerk to the Taunton Rural District Council, explained that, *the District Council had constantly been receiving complaints of the shortage of water in Bishops*

The stream at the lowest point of Mount Street below Rodney Cottage (now Captain's Cottage).
This stream had right- angled bends at both ends and these caused it to flood in heavy rain. On the waters receding frogs were left strewn across the road, hence the name Frog Street.

In 1976 the course of the stream was changed. A new course was cut to carry the water straight on after flowing under Mount Street. A culvert was laid along the old line of the stream to drain water. This now lies under the front gardens of 41 a-e Mount Street.

Lydeard for the last 12 to 14 years and at the present time one ratepayer had not been able to get any water at his house for six weeks. He went on to say, the council had examined the supply some years ago but found there was no way of increasing it as Mr. Esdaile had no other spring which could be connected to the present supply. We then went to Bagborough with the object of getting a supply from the springs there but we were unable to accept the terms proposed by the agent of the owner.

Mr. Dawe continued, *Now that Colonel Boles has bought the property, he has offered to give the District Council permission to take the water from the springs to supply Bagborough and Bishops Lydeard, through his lands, for the nominal sum of ten shillings per year, provided that his house and cottages are supplied free of water rates. I consider this a very generous offer as there will be a great saving in labour in bringing the pipes across Colonel Boles' land.*

The Chairman, Mr. Esdaile, enquired as to the cost of the scheme. Mr. Dawe replied, *the total estimated cost of this scheme, with a 10,000 gallon storage tank and a 2 inch main pipe would be £4500, of which Bagborough would pay £800. A 3 inch pipe would cost an extra £1800 and should this meeting recommend a larger storage tank it would cost £220 for each extra 10,000 gallons.* He concluded, *the present supply does not meet Ministry of Health requirements, as a water supply should be 15 gallons per head per day.*

At this point Colonel Boles got to his feet and addressed the meeting. *There seems to be a feeling among some people in the village that this scheme is being promoted in my interest. I wish to make it quite clear to them that if they do not require the water, then I do not wish it on them. The object of my offer is that I have always had the best interest of Bishops Lydeard at heart and have always been willing to do the Parish a good turn. I should be very pleased for them to have the water if they require it.*

The debate continued with Mr. Lambson saying, *having heard Mr. Dawe's explanation of the scheme and the requirements of the Ministry of Health, I have not the slightest doubt that the additional supply is required to maintain the health of the Parish.*

Mr. Simons and Mr. Welch both remarked that they considered that if the present supply was used for domestic purposes only, then there would be plenty of water available. Mr. Wright got to his feet and angrily informed them, *I suggest you come and live at the top end of the village and you would soon find out that there is a shortage.*

Mr. Shattock agreed, *I have lived at The Buildings for several years and have experienced great difficulty in getting water. Often I cannot get water after 8 o'clock in the morning.*

Finally the proposal was made that Colonel Boles' offer be accepted and that a 20,000 gallon storage tank should be built. This was carried by sixteen votes to two.

The Bishops Lydeard Fire Brigade.

In 1898 an order was put in for one Merryweather and Sons improved Hand and Hose Cart - Twickenham pattern - made of well-seasoned hardwood, capable of carrying 1000 feet of hose and with a covered toolbox in front to take a standpipe, spanners etc. The cart to be mounted on a pair of high spoke wheels with steel springs and a dragging handle for men. Painted in vermillion and black. 700 feet of woven canvas hose to be supplied which will be oak bark tanned by our own patent process. The cost £54 .13 .6d, delivered free.

In January 1899 Walter Hanks was made captain of a brigade of five men. The men he selected to act with him were Henry Newton, Harry Saunders, William Saunders, John Yandell and John Mullins. The appliance was kept in a shed rented from Mr. Hartnell for £2 .15s a year. Unfortunately, due to ill health, Walter Hanks resigned in January 1900 and Henry Newton was made Captain.

The following rules were adopted for the fire brigade:

Rule 1- that the brigade consists of a captain and five men, one of which shall be the water manager.

Rule 2 - the captain will have the responsibility of maintaining a thoroughly efficient brigade and he shall be in sole command of the brigade when on duty. In all matters however the brigade shall be subject to the decision of the Bishops Lydeard Parish Council.

Rule 3 - all orders given by the captain are to be executed with prompt obedience. Any member of the brigade misbehaving himself or disobeying orders will forfeit his pay. No smoking will be allowed when on duty. On receiving notice, all members must hasten to the fire brigade station. When about to leave for a fire, all appliances must be called over and a search made for any missing part.

Rule 4 - all members of the brigade shall meet quarterly for practice on the day appointed by the captain. The practice shall not be less than one and a half hours including the taking out and replacing of the appliance. The men shall be paid one shilling for each time they attend.

Rule 5 - the pay when called to a fire shall be for the captain two shillings for the first hour and one shilling per hour afterwards, and 1/6d per hour for the men for the first hour and 9d per hour after. The higher rates of pay will not be given to men arriving one hour late.

The first fire attended by the brigade occurred in Frog Street on 10th April 1906 when a row of seven cottages were gutted. The fire began at 4:30 pm in the roof of the cottage on the left. The Taunton Fire Brigade was also called by a telegram, taking 30 minutes to arrive. Both brigades fought the blaze until midnight, fortunately nobody was hurt and most people managed to save their possessions. The Taunton Brigade went off with two 50 ft lengths of hose belonging to Bishops

The remains of the cottages in Frog Street after the big blaze of 1906

Lydeard. The cost to the Parish Council of the fire was £2 .3 .6d.

On 14th November 1912 a fire occurred at the house of Walter Yandell and the brigade was called. The captain received 9/6d to distribute in payment.

The fire station had been in Mr. Hartnell's shed and after this fire he asked for an increase in rent to £3 .15s a year. The Parish Council decided to inform Mr. Hartnell, on 19th March 1913, that the appliance would be removed early the following week and placed temporarily in Walter Darby's barn, unless he consented to continue the tenancy of the station on the same terms as before and also repair the roof. The appliance was removed! A new fire station was eventually located in Mr. Newton's shed.

The Parochial Church Council, in January 1921, asked if the fire appliances were manned and in good working order. During the War most of the men were called up and the captain had resigned. The Parish Council had been unable to fill the vacancies. The hose was leaky and would require great expenditure to put it in working order. Two years later it was agreed that Mr. Wright be appointed captain at five shillings a practice and Messrs. Salter, Young and Welch be paid 2/6d a practice.

It was another 13 years, on 24th October 1936, before the brigade was called out again to attend a chimney fire in Church Street. Only two lengths of hose were found to be usable, the remainder being perished, the stopcocks were choked with grit, in consequence it was a considerable time before any water was available. It was also noted that the appliance was being stored outside in the open and not in the shed rented from Mr. Newton.

As the Taunton Fire Brigade stated that they could be at Bishops Lydeard in approximately 10 minutes, if summoned, a decision was made in 1937 to disband the Bishops Lydeard Fire Brigade. The appliance was sold to Taunton for £2 .10s.

The War Years
1914 - 1918

German and Austrian Officers leaving Bishops Lydeard station on their way to internment in Sandhill Park. Fifty arrived on 16th December 1916 and a further sixty on 26th March 1917.

Gladys Palmer was eleven at the end of the Great War but remembered life in the village as if it were yesterday!

Many of the men-folk went off to war during the first year [some 110 in fact]. *Mr. Welch had five sons joining the colours. Dr. Frossard's eldest son, Charles, a second Lieutenant with the Devonshires had been wounded and been returned to hospital in Torquay. His youngest son, Hugh, Lieutenant in the Marines, was wounded in the Dardanelles.*

In the summer 1915 a lot of soldiers arrived at Sandhill for training and the village became very busy. [Two companies of the Army Services Corps, some 600 men, under Lieutenant Spoor]. *Later Sandhill was used to house Prisoners of War. They were German and Austrian officers who often used to swagger around the village, presumably under guard.*

I remember the Royal Visit very well. [7th - 8th September 1915]. *The station had never looked so tidy since the day it opened. The coal trucks were removed and the stacks of coal were neatly covered with tarpaulin sheets. Each side of the siding had been carefully rolled and gravelled. Some lamps had been put up and even a telephone installed. Crowds gathered outside the station on the grass, with picnics, to meet the 6:10 pm train. Some had come from a long distance but were not allowed to stay to see the train. The church bells were rung to greet their Majesties.*

[The King and Queen had come to rest after a long day in Bristol visiting wounded soldiers in several hospitals. The following day they went to Exeter and Plymouth to review troops and visit the wounded. They did not leave the train on that Tuesday evening but early on the Wednesday morning a few people were able to see them walking around the station yard].

We children were very lucky. We were marched down from school with our teachers and the vicar and let straight on to the station platform. We lined up a few feet from the carriages and sang the National Anthem. We were told to cheer loudly as the train pulled out [at 10:15 am] *and the King and Queen waved from their window, although I don't remember them smiling! Afterwards we marched back to the Gore Inn, sang the National Anthem, and had the rest of the day as a holiday.*

The village did things to help the War Effort. Many articles were made in the village which Mrs. Benson, at Lydeard House, collected and got passed to the West Somersets. I remember there was a collection at school for money to supply plum puddings for the Somerset men at the front. Mrs. Boles, at Watts House, appealed for khaki bags to be made. [Each bag was filled with a cake of carbolic soap, a tin of dubbin, vaseline, boot laces, cigarettes, notepaper, envelopes and a pencil, together with St. Matthews Gospel].

Other things which we children did were to collect whortleberries on the Hills which were turned into dye for naval uniforms. We also picked acorns, mace as we used to call them, and conkers. The headmaster, Mr. Bunston, organized the collection and storage in the Bell Assembly Rooms. [Fourteen and a half hundredweight were collected in the village to be used in the production of munitions, instead of grain. In the country overall 5000 tons were collected in 1917, saving 2000 tons of grain, equivalent to 3,700,000 loaves of bread!].

I never remember us starving during the War but we were often very hungry. There was a man that came out from Taunton once a week. Everyone called him Moses. He was a funny little man, he had a bicycle with hooks on the side and always wore a black straw hat. He sold faggots and peas which we used to boil up and eat.

Every week in the summer another man came out with a horse and float to sell ice cream. A cornet cost $^1/_2d$. We had eight weeks holiday at the end of June to work in the hayfields and 1918 was a very good harvest and I remember the boys from King's College in Taunton camping near the Gore Inn and working on the farms throughout August.

The day the War ended there were flags in most windows of the houses and on each of the corners of the church tower, from which the bells rang. There was a big bonfire by the Girl Guide Hut and a dance in the Working Men's Institute during the evening.

The church tower had been an indirect casualty of the War. A village meeting had been called in June 1914 to discuss the condition of the pinnacles and parapets of the tower. The vicar said that the corrosion of the iron stays and clamps had done much damage resulting in the stonework being in a dangerous condition. The lead flashing needed completely replacing. The cost of the work would be approximately £400. Another meeting in August was called but adjourned until the following Saturday, because "of the possibility of war breaking out between this country and Germany in the next few days".

War did break out and the work on the tower did not proceed but Messrs. H. J. Spiller and Son were instructed to make it as safe as possible for the duration of the war. In 1918 Spiller's reported the parapet on the south aisle was now dangerous, roof timbers had decayed and part of the north side pinnacle had just fallen off. Work had to be put in hand immediately and fundraising started, with several promises of substantial assistance being given.

In 2004 St. Mary's Church finds itself in a similar situation. The cost however is not £500 but £500,000!

Repairs to the church tower by H. J. Spiller.
The two gentlemen on top of the tower are, on the left, the new vicar Rev Fitch, who arrived in 1919, and Mr George Axe, sidesman.

The War Memorial

A Parish Meeting was held on 7th February 1919 under the chairmanship of the vicar, the Reverend Whately, to discuss what kind of War Memorial would be most suitable for the Parish.

The following people made these proposals:

Mr. Doble - a stone monument with names thereon.

Mr. Hearn - a lychgate at the churchyard.

Colonel Boles - a recreation ground, lychgate or village hall.

Mr Esdaile - a drinking fountain for men and beasts.

Mrs. Esdaile - a stone cross.

Mr. Webber - a recreation ground.

Mr. Saunders - a stone inside of the churchyard with names thereon.

Mr. Badcock - an arch and new gates to the churchyard with a tablet and names on it.

Voting was then taken on these proposals with the following results:

The Stone Monument 3 votes, Lychgate or Stone Arch with new gates at the church 39 votes, Recreation Ground 19 votes, Village Hall 13 votes, a Stone inside the churchyard 3 votes.

A committee was formed to report to a future Parish Meeting. It reported in April 1919 that a village hall, even if the large amount required was subscribed, its upkeep would be an unfair burden on the Parish. A recreation ground was not possible as they had unsuccessfully endeavoured to obtain a site. However, although a recreation site was a necessity, it should not be obtained as a War Memorial. A plan had been drawn up for a lychgate or arch and this was circulated. A likely cost would be £300 and it was agreed that tenders be advertised for this project.

Captain Benson reported the following month that tenders had been received of between £400 and £500. This was more than the £300 for which the architects had been instructed to prepare plans. The committee decided that this project was therefore impracticable.

The War Memorial in Mount Street as it was originally constructed. The steps were removed when the wall was moved back in the 1980's.

This left the idea of a cross inside the gates of the churchyard as the last remaining suitable form of a memorial. The committee was empowered to get plans and quotations for this.

A large number of people attended the meeting on 25th November 1919, when three designs were presented costing from £127 to £160. The design, in Ham Hill stone, costing £160 was adopted and a site for the cross was then discussed. These were, at the crossroads opposite the new police station [West Street], in the garden at the entrance to Halfyard Lane [Quantock View] or at the entrance to Mill Lane. Finally, however, it was carried by a large majority to place it in the churchyard and have all the names of those men who served in the Army and Navy during the War, and those who laid down their lives, inscribed upon it.

The last recorded evidence on the construction of the Memorial was on 30th April 1920. Colonel Boles had offered a site in Frog Street for the cross and Captain Benson had ordered the cross from the Ham Hill Stone Company. A meeting was called at Watts House to make out a list of the fallen whose names should be inscribed on the cross.

There is no record of how the War Memorial actually came to be erected in Mount Street. It was unveiled on 23rd January 1921 at 2:30pm by Lt. Col. Hartley Maud and dedicated by The Bishop of Bath and Wells.

A poignant reminder of the "War to end all Wars" can be seen in the little group of war graves in the churchyard. On the 25th January 1917 Private William

The War Memorial unveiling cermony on 23rd January 1921.

Yandell, of the Royal Fusiliers, was the first soldier who had fallen, to be buried in the village. He had only been in France for six weeks before being wounded in the arm and shoulder. After four months in English hospitals he died in Manchester. Soldiers from Taunton Barracks marched to the village to act as bearers and fired three rounds over the grave and a bugler sounded "Last Post".

The War Years
1939 - 1945

Don Saunders. *During the war most male workers were away. Gordon Skinner, up at Pound Farm, had two Land Girls, Diana and Mavis. Gerald Hawkins and I used to go up there hoeing out the yellow weed in the corn, acres and acres of it. At 5pm we used to knock on the door and we were greeted by, "Are you sure you've done your work, what do I have to give you, 1/6d?" "No," I said, "we've done five hours, that's half a crown." Half a crown for a whole afternoon's work!*

Sometimes, in the summer, we used to go up to Ulick Huntington at Heathersett, two or three times a week, picking and sorting potatoes and apples again at 6d an hour. One couldn't get better pay than that.

When I was fourteen I left school to work in the Buffer Depot for 25 shillings a week. A London firm built sheds down by the station to store food for the Ministry of Food. Food, like corn beef, was stored in the sheds and every so often a train would come into the siding, by the sheds, at 11am. Most of the time we were scratching around for something to do. Just beyond the sheds Farmer Bolt had a piece of land [where the toilets now are]. He came down one day and said, as far as he was concerned, we could have the land as it would save him cutting it. So the seven of us, who were working in the Depot, had a plot of ground each on which we were able to work whilst waiting for a train to come in. The Red Cross train would come into the station and twenty or more ambulances would take the wounded soldiers up to the hospital.

Major Bicknell, in Orchard Lea, ran the ARP. He had a veranda on the front which had two beds and a telephone for the two who were on duty for the night. He also organized the evacuees from London.

The skittle alley at the Bell Inn was converted into a Rest House for Air Raid Wardens from London. They had beds upstairs and easy chairs downstairs. Most would go back after a month or so.

We were all fitted with gas masks in square boxes with string to hang over our shoulder. The masks were made of rubber - and did they smell!

Usually the American soldiers had drunk all the beer in the pubs by Wednesday and so went on to cider. They

Major Bicknell of Orchard Lea. The Major ran the ARP and organised the evacuees from London during Second World War

never appreciated how strong it was, so the Military Police, in their white helmets, were always coming down and hauling the soldiers into the jeep.

My friend Micky Forward [son of the landlord of the Bell Inn] *and I used to walk up Whisky Trail to the wall on Sandhill. We used to say over the wall to the soldiers, "Have you got any gum, chum?" They used to reply, "Do you want any cigarettes - Lucky Strike, Camel or whatever". They used to chuck these over and say, "Can you get us any beer?" Well, if Micky's dad had any in the pub we used to take up bottles of beer and sometimes they even gave us a £5 note. They had so much money, they couldn't spend it all.*

Mary Bird. *The Americans were always good to the kids in the village, usually throwing out cigarettes or 'candy' from the trucks as they drove through. They put on good parties for us at Sandhill. Your name would be called out to go and get a present.*

I remember one nasty incident. I was taking the dog for a walk, with my friend, when we were asked by the Military Police if we had seen a big black man in a dressing gown. We had, because he had stopped to stroke the dog. We were told later he had jumped from a tree up Cherry Isle [Watts Lane]. *We were always scared to go up there after that.*

Gladys Palmer. *During the Second World War we used to barter food. If one liked cheese and another didn't then they used to swap for something they liked. My brother-in-law, Raymond, registered as an agricultural worker - he was really a groom for the Bole's - so he didn't go in the war. All agricultural workers had an extra ration of cheese, so he often let me have some and I swapped with our neighbour for some tea.*

We lived at Halfyard in the war and the German planes used to fly over on their way to Port Talbot. One night a row of incendiaries was dropped in the gardens. The men ran out in their pyjamas putting them out. The only other occasion the village suffered bombing was when two bombs fell in the field beside Taunton Road.

The village received the first influx of soldiers in August 1940 when the British 41st General Military Hospital was set up at Sandhill. When the British were moved to the Middle East, in 1941, the hospital was leased to the American government as a neurological hospital for 1000 patients. One hundred brick and concrete structures were built, including 32 wards. The mansion itself was used for the medical staff.

It was certainly excusable that most villagers were excited in the early days by the sight of soldiers in uniform walking in the country lanes or the searchlights in the fields sweeping the skies at night. The pubs were the obvious meeting place for troops and villagers. There were regularly organized dances and events for everyone to mix. However, there were a few 'silly young women' who developed 'street corner' relationships with the soldiers with the inevitable consequences! Certainly the village became aware of racial differences for the first time. Black soldiers who went out with the village girls were treated badly and fights often broke out at dances. Most villagers generally did not share this prejudice and it was true that most black GI's were very polite and well-mannered.

The other influx into the village was some 50 children evacuated from London. They were the first to use the newly completed Village Hall, in 1939. Major Bicknell headed a committee to organize their billeting and the majority of these children adjusted to the way of life in the country but some did not and returned to London.

It is probably true to say that most villagers, as a result of the war, obtained a greater insight into race relations and inner city life. However they did not experience the hardships of bombing or suffer greatly due to food rationing.

The aftermath of war did not prevent village dissention occurring. On 1st May 1946 it was decided to celebrate Victory Day and a large committee, including all the Parish Council, was set up to make the arrangements.

It was necessary to call a special village meeting on the 15th May to settle differences between the authorized and unauthorized organizers. Mr. Darby stated that it would be a calamity to celebrate victory with strife. The vicar, John du Boulay Lance, said that he and others coming home from service considered the disunity a disgraceful affair and that it should be possible for the two parties to work together. Mr. Manderson, the leader for the unauthorized body, declared he had no faith in the Parish Council and explained what he and those with him were doing for Victory Day.

It was impossible to reconcile the opposing sides and a vote was taken as to which body should proceed with the arrangements. Mr. Manderson and his group won.

Bishops Lydeard Tales

The Wagon Maker's Wife - Mrs. Florence Woollen

Florence was born in Street but came to work in Bishops Lydeard, as a nurse at Sandhill, in 1929. At the time of writing she still lives in Church Street, aged 95 years.

At that time there were only female patients, separated into the under 16's, with their own school, and the over 16's. Men came later and worked in the gardens - there was a gardener and a cowman who lived either side of the lodge. We nurses used to train the patients to look after themselves and do housework. I would do three months in the kitchen with the cook, then on to the laundry with the laundress and then to the sick wards under the matron. The patients were trained to keep the hospital clean. Some patients went to work in the village, particularly in Watts House and Lydeard House.

The gardens at Sandhill Park

I married Mr. Parkman, my first husband, in 1936. His father kept the shop [now the Fruit and Veg. Shop], as a grocer and bootmaker. After my husband died I went back for two years to Street before returning to marry Jack Woollen, in 1939. He was a regular in the RAF and when he was in Palestine his parents William and Elizabeth Woollen moved from Bagborough into the house called The Bartons.

William had started his business at Bagborough as a carpenter and wheelwright, and moved to The Bartons, with its big yard, to expand the business. He made farm wagons, wheelbarrows and mended traps, for which Elizabeth did the upholstery. William was also the undertaker before Mr. Back took over. The house was at the top of the yard and in the yard there was a smithy, carpenter and paint shops. Unfortunately William had gangrene and had to have a leg removed and strangely his wife, who had, since she was young, been troubled with a bad leg also had to have it removed. My father-in-law lived to 86 and Elizabeth outlived him.

Everyone was sociable and they knew each other. The old folk in the almshouses used to bring their chairs outside and chat as people went by. People looked after each other, they didn't need social workers.

William Woollen at Bagborough with a caravan he had made.

Left. The house called The Bartons can be seen at the end of the yard. A typical waggon made at W. H. Woollens can be seen in the yard

Right. William Woollen completing a wheel for a waggon.

Mr. Wilton, on the left and Mr. King in the blacksmith shop.

*Below. Jack Woollen sold the land to Van Heusen's around 1956 and they built their factory in the yard.
Eventually the house, The Bartons, was burned down to make way for the houses which were built on the site.*

The Saddler's Daughter - Miss Phyllis Axe

Phyllis Axe was born in 1911 and attended the village school and Bishop Fox's. Her father, George Axe, had married Anne Lockyer and they moved from Salisbury to Bishops Lydeard to take over the saddlemaker's business from Mr Trickey around 1908. Phyllis had two older brothers, Stanley and Alwyne. Sadly, in 1914, Stanley had a fall from the ropes in the gym at Huish School, hitting his head badly. A few days later he died, aged 14. His grave can be seen in the Churchyard, on the right, just inside the gate. Alwyne joined Lloyd's Bank and, despite suffering from multiple sclerosis from his early 30s, worked beyond retirement age and died in 1978, aged 73. Phyllis went into teaching in Birmingham from 1931 - 71, reaching two headships. She now lives in Evesham.

My father was a sidesman at St Mary's, a member of the Parish Council, a school manager, a trustee of the almshouses and secretary of the Conservative Association. As secretary, when Colonel Boles and later Colonel Gault were elected to Parliament, it was the custom for my father to supply ropes and he and friends met the MP's car at the Gore Inn, fastened the ropes and pulled the car up the village to the committee rooms.

My father had a second shop at Crowcombe. As Thursday was half day closing in Bishops Lydeard, he spent all day at Crowcombe leaving the Bishops Lydeard shop in the charge of his assistant. He drove to Crowcombe in a horse and trap and in the holidays often took me with him. Today the shop is Saddler's Cottage.

Left. George Axe outside his saddlemakers shop now 9 Church Street, c. 1913.

Middle. Alwyne and Phyllis Axe c. 1914.

Right. Stanley Axe in his scout uniform.

I don't have many memories of the First War. I recall soldiers going to war and many not returning. One local vicar, Reverend Sperway, had three of his four sons killed. German POW's sometimes marched, escorted, through the village and I can see them playing football at Sandhill. I was lucky to be on the platform to see the King and Queen and was amazed to see the Queen in a carriage furnished like a sitting room and the King next door in a similar one. They came to the window to acknowledge our cheers.

I do remember the May Day celebrations, in 1919. Beautiful arches were built across the village street and it poured with rain. On May Day we always danced around the maypole.

At school we sat in the long desks holding about five children. The school bell rang at 8.55 and 1.25 each day, five minutes before school started. By the time I left, Mr. Tipper was headmaster and Miss Hanks was his assistant. From 1923 - 28, I went to Bishop Fox's on the Minehead to Taunton train. We were never allowed to mix schools and certainly not to sit with the boys. During the General Strike of 1926, Mrs. Webber drove her family and me to school as the were no trains running to Taunton. The first village bus, I recall, had a long seat each side, open to the air with tarpaulins which could be lowered in bad weather. Passengers had to walk up a couple of steps at the back and entered through a little door. Mr. Percy Hanks drove the bus and when the passengers were seated, his father closed the door and always rode outside on the top step, unless the weather was too inclement. In 1928, Mr. Hanks decided to run a school bus from Bishops Lydeard. We all used to use it and mixed with the boys! I had the invaluable experience in writing lines given by various teachers -it was customary to write out 500 times 'I must not talk'!

Entertainments were very different from today. My first 'Magic Lantern Show' was one evening, viewing The Garden City of Bourneville, sitting on top of a desk in the schoolroom. (I did not know then that I should be motoring daily through Bourneville on my way to work, many years later). Occasionally a tent was erected in a field near the station, in the summertime, for a Marionette Show - seats were priced at 2d.

The games we played indoors were ludo, snakes and ladders, dominoes, draughts, whist and other card games. Outdoors we did a lot of skipping, hop scotch, tops, walking and when we were older, cycling and tennis. When large wagons stopped in the village overnight in Bell Green, we used to somersault over the wooden shafts of the wagon. We used to call this timpintailling!

The meetings of horse and hounds were very popular especially on Boxing Day. They met at the Bell Inn in West Street opposite our house. There was always an interesting collection of riders of all shapes and sizes in addition to the regular huntsmen. Fetes, gymkhanas and point to point were all part of village enjoyment. In the autumn a ploughing match was held with the local farm labourers competing. In the evening a supper was held at the Bell Hotel. My father and other men shared the task of carving the joints of meat.

Sunday School was held at 10.15 am in the school and then we walked in twos to the church for morning service. At 3 pm we had Children's Service in the church. Sunday School outings were held to Watchet, Minehead or Weston. I preferred Weston because there were donkeys to ride on the sands.

On Rogation Sunday, after evening service, the vicar, choir and congregation walked from church to Mr. Bolt's wheatfield beyond the Gore Inn. After the vicar climbed into a farm cart to address us we lustily sang hymns.

It was the custom to toll the church bell when someone died. This was followed by three tolls for a man and four for a woman, so you always knew the sex of the deceased.

I remember 'Johny Fortnight' who came to the village once a fortnight with his travelling bag selling tape, elastic, needles, pins and darning wool.

There was also the lamplighter who in the winter carried his ladder, rested it on the arms at the top of the lamp post and lit the wick inside. One of the lamps was outside our house. In 1928 electricity came to the village after many people sponsored the plan, my father being one of them. The street lamps were switched on at The Gore, attended by the Parish Council. We needed thirteen lights in our house but my mother refused to have such an unlucky number, so we only had twelve. We never had a light in the larder!

George Axe inside the shop c. 1945

George Lovell, grandfather of Fred Lovell, outside Swan Cottage.

The Grocer's Daughter - Mrs. Pat Lathbury

Pat was born Pat Lovell, in 1915, in Swan Cottage and lives in Hither Mead, at the time of writing.

My father, Fred Lovell, was born in 1883 in Combe Florey, but was brought up by his grandparents who lived in Swan Cottage. He left school at 14 and went to work in Mr. Cook's shop (now the Co-op). In 1900 he started his own grocery business in one room of Swan Cottage. When he first started he used to take in mushrooms and blackberries which people had picked, then harness the horse and cart at 4 - 5 am and take them into Taunton. He would come back with a box of kippers for the villagers to buy.

My mother was lady's maid to Lady Alianore Lethbridge. She became very close to Lady Alianore and the three children Tory, Dulcie and Hector. When Lady Alianore returned from a holiday to India, she brought mother back some beaded sandal shoes and a necklace. Gossip said that Alianore had been 'involved' with an Indian Prince and hence the divorce from Sir Wroth in 1911.

My father and mother married in 1913. When War came and my father served in the army, mother had to run the business. She had a very good girl to help her, who used to deliver the groceries in the horse and trap. In winter she would come back with her skirts frozen!

Mr. Berry, a wholesale grocer in Bridgwater, was very friendly with my father. The house where Mrs. Ashman ran her little shop, was bought by Mr. Berry and we were able to move in from Swan Cottage. Eventually my parents bought the house.

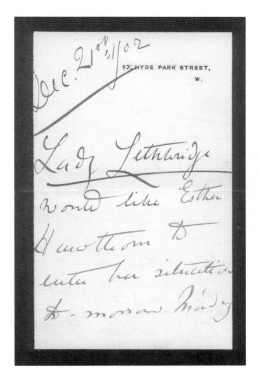

Above. Lady Alianore Lethbridge in 1907 and the letter she wrote to Pat's mother inviting her to become her maid(1902).

Our shop, on the end of the house, had a wonderful smell of spices. As you went in through the door, from Mount Street, in front of you was a marble counter on which there was butter, lard, cheese in big blocks and bacon. To the right there was a mahogany counter underneath which was kept all the sugar. The sugar came direct from Tate and Lyle and had to bagged up into 2 lb bags. Behind the counter were big drawers with brass handles and shelves above them. In the far right-hand corner there were two steps up to the kitchen and the bottom step was made of wood under which my father kept the cash box. Big sides of bacon had to be boned and sliced. Hams were cooked and hung in a little tiled alcove by the door up to the kitchen. A staircase at the back of the shop led up to the storeroom. When the big boxes of dates arrived we had to use an old screwdriver to get them out to sell. Sultanas also came in big boxes. All the groceries for delivery were packed up in brown paper parcels and tied up with string.

Rabbit was the most popular meat between the wars and during the Second War. A rabbit could be bought for 2d or 3d and a skin could be sold for a 1d at 'Lovells'. Getting a bill paid was always difficult - people bought things on 'tick' - they always owed my father. He had boys working for him and used to say. "Don't leave the groceries unless you get the money." When a boy returned, father would ask. "Where's the money from Mrs. So and so?" The boy would reply. "Oh, she started to cry so I had to let her have them." My father said he could have retired on the interest

Lovells Stores in Mount Street, now Lovells Cottage. Before Fred Lovell moved in it was Mrs Ashman's General Stores and prior to that it was a pub called The Dove Inn.

on the money owed him! Another job the boys had to do was to empty the bucket in the outside lavatory. They emptied it under the apple tree and those apples were beautiful - big red quarrenders. The tree eventually died and gooseberries and blackberries were planted there. They were also beautiful being 'so well oiled'!! We never had food left over, it would all go. During the Second War gypsies would camp on Ash Priors Common with caravans and horses. They would come in and have all the odd bits of bacon and cheese.

My father suffered from Parkinsons and died in 1940. I had married Frank (Lathbury) and with my mother kept the shop going. When my mother died, in 1971, Frank and I decided to close 'Lovells Stores' and retire.

The Lovell Family. Fred, Esther and Pat.

The Carter's Daughter - Mrs. Mary Bird

I was born in one of the cottages beyond the almhouses. They have been demolished since to build The Bartons houses. Mr. and Mrs. Wright lived on one side and an old man lived the other, he was always buying and drinking cider from Greed's Store. The cottage had a sitting room entered from the street and in it was a coal fire with a copper boiler on one side. At the back was a scullery with a sink and then a small yard with steps up to the allotment. We had three small bedrooms, each the size of a box room nowadays.

My father, Sydney Gillard, when he left school at fourteen, worked as a stoker boy on W.J. King's steam tractors. He used to cook eggs and bacon on a shovel in the fire of the boiler.

W. J. King's 'Little Giant' type compound steam wagon of 1924

After he was married he worked as Mr. Darby's delivery man taking the corn meal by horse and cart to the outlying farms. One day, I remember, Mum had bought some doughnuts from Kilford's. Dad had popped in for a cup of tea. The doughnuts were hot so Mum had put them on the windowsill to cool. Darling, the horse, standing outside, put his head through the open window and ate them!

As a girl at the school, I recall writing on slates and making models out of clay. We had a cookery teacher called Miss Seymour. Cooking lessons were held in the Guide Hut. We were taught about the Hay Box. This was a tea chest filled with hay and when a stew was carefully packed in it, the stew kept hot for ages. A knife was used to scrape dust from a brick and this brick dust was used to clean the scum from an enamel bath. We also cooked 'Scrumps' - flap jacks - which we took home for tea. My favourite teacher was Miss Wells. She was like a caring Aunt, if you went to sleep she put a pillow under your head!

Mary Bird, front left, at work in Van Heusen's Factory at Sandhill Park, before the new factory was bulit at The Bartons.

W. J. King quarrying operation at Triscombe Quarry in the Quantock Hills.

Page 160. Logging in the Quantocks using steam power.

The Schoolmistress - Mrs. Gladys Palmer

Gladys was born, Gladys Saunders, in a cottage beside the Bird in Hand Pub, in 1907.

My father, Henry Saunders, worked for 42 years, on commission for Prudential, cycling around the villages selling insurance. There were five of us children. My eldest brother, Jack, went as a page boy to Cothelstone House and my eldest sister, Rose, was a scullery maid to Sir Wroth and Lady Lethbridge.

Gladys Palmer c. 1925

I started school at the age of three, walking up Mount Street from the cottage. As we passed The Mount, the maid, Mabel Upham, used to throw apples down to us from the side window. There was little traffic about in those days. On the left, around the corner was Mrs. Ashman's little general store - later Fred Lovell's store. I used to go into Ashman's to buy halfpenny worth of sweets on my way to school. Amy Ashman was extremely cross-eyed so you were never sure which eye to look into! She would wrap a piece of paper round her hand to make a cone, turn up the bottom and put the sweets in. I sometimes had to buy a halfpenny dummy, which I put under my pinafore and if I was put in the corner at school I used to take out my dummy and suck it.

In school we used to write on slates, the chalk often used to screech when we wrote and we cleaned them off with spit and a sponge! Mr. Simons was headmaster and I remember being frightened to death when he caned the same boy in all four classrooms, as a lesson to everybody else. The boys name was Arthur Shabley who lived at Cotford. There was Miss Timber, in the Infant Room, who was extremely tall and in a kid's eyes looked like a giant. Miss Gardiner in the next room taught us to sew. We used to make chemises and shirts for charity, all hand-sewn as there were no machines. During the First War there were several retired men who came to teach. Mr. Masklyn was evil, he used to put a penknife under your hand to make you write properly. If you dropped your hand you felt the blade. Mr. Bunston lived at Kingston St. Mary and came in by train each day. He was sadistic giving both boys and girls a wallop that would send you right across the room! He did so to me once for fooling around and not doing my arithmetic.

When we lived at 'Roseneath' next door to us was Tiny Pearce - a big man, who was the blacksmith and I loved to watch him making shoes for the horses. Around the corner was Mr. Doble, the carpenter and wheelwright. Tiny used to bond the metal hoops on to the wheels and then fill a watering can from the big water tank and pour the water all round the wheel. We kids were thrilled to bits watching the wheels sizzle! When shoeing horses he always put the nails in his mouth and we were afraid he would swallow them. Tiny also sharpened the scythes for the farmers on a huge grindstone outside, making sparks fly.

As children we often went down the lanes or up on the hills picking things. Crolick Lane (opposite the football field) *was good for mushrooms. Violets and primroses were picked every Good Friday, from Terhill Lane. While in season whortleberries were picked. At 6 am we went through Crolick Lane, up the long lane to Bagborough, then up the steep slope of Stout Lane, beside the Rising Sun, to the stream and spring.* (It was this water which was used later to supply our village). *We did this each day while the berries lasted much to the annoyance of one old lady up at Bagborough who called us 'those old Lydeardites'. 'Trug' Rich used to come over the hills in a pony and trap and call out "whorts, whorts" and we children were paid 4d a quart. (A Birds Eye custard tin would hold about a pint of whorts).*

During the First War our family moved from 'Roseneath' to Surgery House (now Birch House in Church Street) *to act as caretaker for Dr Frossard and the Church Rooms. Dr Frossard used to mix up his own medicines from his corked glass bottles and then leave them on the table in the surgery. I often had to clean his pestle and mortar. He mainly dispensed, however, castor oil and bicarbonate of soda which seemed to cure most ills! Most of his patients were so poor he did not charge them, so he himself was often in debt.*

My mother died in Surgery House leaving enough from insurance to bury her and, with the little that was left over, Dad bought a wireless. It was a little black box with two coils at the back which you adjusted with a lever to tune it and it just fitted on the window ledge. When King George V was ill, Dr Frossard would come down from surgery at lunchtime to Dad to find out about the King's health. "How is he today, Harry," he would say in his broken English - he came from the Channel Islands. He

Dr. and Mrs. Frossard

knew Lord Dawson Penn, the King's surgeon and had little time for him. Dr Frossard
always used to laugh at the diagnosis and say. "Give him a drop more whisky."
Mother always made sure we had a good Christmas. Paper trimmings were hung in
one room and paper lanterns in another. The children always drank Stones Ginger
Wine in the room with the lanterns and the adults in the other room drank port wine.
Sometimes the lanterns would catch fire and Dad would come in and blow them out.
The Madrigal Society had been formed by Mr. Tipper and on Christmas Eve toured
the village in Percy Hank's bus. The route was always the same, from Dene Court to
W.J. King's at Tatham, on to the Lethbridge to sing behind the bar, then The Bird in
Hand followed by The Bell. Mrs. Vernon always had a punch bowl waiting in the hall
for us at Lydeard House and from there on to Watts House where, if we not on time,
we would get no answer. By then it would often be after midnight and we would go
on to Dr Cornish at Pixford Farm. He would always come down to us in his pyjamas
and give us sandwiches. We would finish in Gore Square on Christmas morning.
Mr. Tipper, apart from being headmaster and a reporter for the Somerset County
Gazette, was also church organist and choirmaster. During the 1920's there were
some thirty in the choir who practiced twice a week. Sundays were always taken up,
by all ages, in going to church - there was nothing else to do! The church was always
packed, everyone had their own pew. Communion was at 8 am. - the Boles had two
pews half way down the nave on the right and when it was communion nobody, even
his wife, would take communion before Sir Dennis. Sunday School at 10 am. in the
school and morning service at 11 am. Children's service was at 3 pm. when I played
the organ. Evening service was at 6.30 pm., when the back of the church was full of
young boys. Particularly in the summer, after church on a Sunday night, people
would walk down Watts Road and back along New Road to the village - it was known
as 'going round the island'.
At the age of fourteen I took the Pupil Teacher Monitors' Exam. As mother couldn't
afford to send me to college I became an uncertificated teacher and went up to
Cothelstone School to teach. Despite not being trained I became qualified through
service and taught in Bishops Lydeard from 1926 to 1932 when I married Arthur
Palmer. Teacher's pay when I first started was £13 a year and teaching wasn't just
teaching. You used to take off the children's shoes and socks and hang them up to dry!
The school day was 8.45 am. to 4 pm. and children often bought sandwiches for
lunch. When Horlicks started we got in touch with the firm who sent us a cabinet
with trays of mugs and a Horlicks making machine - so the children had Horlicks at
lunchtime. I taught the rest of my career in Taunton.

The Doctor - Dr Philip Woodgate-Jones

The Old Buildings used to house a lot of the staff from Lydeard House and was a wonderful place for swifts to build their nests. They relocated to Mrs. Rank's, Swan Cottage, and one morning I said. "It's lovely to see the swifts have still got a home in your house." She replied. "Oh, but Doctor, they do make an awful mess and I think I shall have to get it boarded up." "You can't do that it's the only place they've got to come to now". Her reply. "Oh well, Doctor, if you says so I won't board it up then."

When I was demobbed I was looking for an opening in general practice. Esme, my wife, had an aunt who knew Dr Fred Blacklee. He telephoned me to say that as his wife had died he was looking to retire at 56. So I arrived in July 1946. Initially I lived with Mrs. Bull at 'Crossways' before moving into Warre Cottage.

Fred Blacklee always liked a drop or two! He always smoked his pipe all through surgery while examining patients. One patient told me. "Dr Blacklee he were a luverly man but he liked a drop you know, Doctor, but when he were like that he knowed more!"

We used to mix up our own medicines. Fred's favourite was Ammonium Picrate which was explosive. I had to order a fresh supply from Ferris's in Bristol and to my surprise a large wooden crate arrived, packed with sawdust, and in the middle was a small bottle of Ammonium Picrate solution. The splendid medicines we made with this - if you coloured it brown, it was known as 'home-brewed' - if you coloured it green it was for nervous dyspepsia and that kind of thing - if you wanted a straight forward tonic you coloured it red! Psychologically this medicine always worked. If the patients got the wrong colour they didn't like it one bit!

The surgery was a little annex at the end of the skittle alley at The Bell. The entrance was from Bell Green - the waiting room came first, then the consulting room with an examination couch, there was no separate examination room. Acoustics weren't terribly good between the consulting room and waiting room, so I had to be careful about what I said or heard under those circumstances.

The Bell Inn. Dr. Woodgate-Jones' surgery was through the door on the right in the Assembly Rooms.

I remember one evening surgery, soon after I arrived, when there were a lot of patients in the waiting room covered in bandages. Apparently there had been an auction in Halse and the floor must have had dry rot. The auctioneer was selling an item and said. "Going, going, gone." Whereupon the floor gave way and they all fell down into the basement. Fortunately most received only minor injuries, apart from one lady with a broken femur, but they said that a large lady living in Halse had fallen on top of them. Well, my last patient that evening was a very large lady and I was able to say. "You must be Mrs. G." She was very surprised. "Yes, Doctor, I am Mrs. G but how did you know?!"

The NHS came in 1948. Up to then we had weekly accounts and send out bills knowing that half would never get paid! In 1951 the practice grew much bigger due the 'squatters' who had moved into Sandhill. It was too large for one person so I wrote to Richard Harrison at my old hospital, Middlesex. He joined me and became a partner in the practice.

Planning permission had been granted to build a surgery in the garden of Warre House. So we built a little surgery with an entrance on to the car park. It was our pride and joy for many years. From the entrance there were two waiting rooms, mine was on the right and Richard's on the left, then through into a consulting room with two examination rooms and a dispensary in the middle. Local opinion had it that if you turned right into my waiting room you got treatment but no diagnosis, if you turned left into Richard Harrison's you got diagnosis but no treatment! So the real crafty patients used to go and rap on the hatch and get to the dispensary direct. Possibly there is a certain amount of truth in it, I'm sure!!

In the early 1970's the Health Centre was built on the south side of the old surgery and they knocked down my 'pride and joy' in just 48 hours! My son, Tim, who had moved into 'West View' joined us and, in 1974, after I had built 'Herrons Reach', he moved into Warre House. When Roger Crabtree came in 1988, I decided to retire and move down to Devon.

On my coming to Bishops Lydeard the District Nurse was Nurse Hunter. She was a super person. She did her rounds on a bicycle which included going up Cothelstone Hill and down the other side. They eventually gave her an Austin Seven which had a 'wheeze' almost as bad as Nurse Hunter's - she used to have terrible colds. She had a very large poodle dog and you were never sure whether she was taking it for a walk or it was taking her! Nurse Hunter eventually moved into the Almshouse where pets were not allowed. I took on a lot of gratuitous jobs during my time and taking on Nurse Hunter's dog was one of them.

Bishops Lydeard had a certain reputation for sizes of families - it was highly competitive. The local obstetrician, Jimmy Thompson, was a very good friend of ours. When women, who consulted him, said they couldn't start a family his final suggestion was that they should move to Bishops Lydeard and that was usually successful!

I acquired a mare, which had been well-bred in the north country by Lord and Lady Ridley. They had been trying to get it in foal but failed. So I wrote to Lady Ridley to tell her that I thought we would get over the trouble now the mare is in Bishops Lydeard, which has a considerable reputation in such matters - however, sad to say, I never got her in foal!!

Ladymead House in Pound Lane was the residence of the Misses Dunn. They were three spinster ladies who were very, very religious. Most people decide on the right house and take a chance on the church. Not the Misses Dunn, they had to have the right churchmanship and then build Ladymead House - they played a terrific part in church life.

Amongst other things they kept a few hens. They always put the date the egg was laid on to it and if it was laid on a Saint's Day they put the name of the Saint on instead. I was called to an old lady one morning and the first thing I ask her was if she had had anything to eat. The reply came. "Yes, Doctor, I had Holy Innocence for breakfast this morning!"

I was called out of the surgery urgently one morning because Frances Dunn had passed out. When I got to Ladymead House there were all three sisters sitting at their breakfast table. Frances was being propped up by Mary on one side and Joanna on the other. Frances was absolutely black obviously having fainted and been propped up by her sisters instead of lying her down. I picked her up and carried her upstairs and put her on her bed. By this time she was bright pink and opened her eyes and said. "Where I be to?" All three sisters eventually died in the village.

Another occasion I was called out one evening to an accident. A man had been drinking in Rose Cottage Inn (latterly The Kingfisher on the A358) and had set off down the road towards Conquest Farm. He got knocked down by a car and when I arrived he was lying in the ditch, in a lot of pain, holding his shoulder. I looked at him and his leg was at a grotesque angle under him. So I said. "What about your leg, isn't that hurting?"

"Oh no, Doctor, that be a wooden leg that be."

He had had his wooden leg knocked off and was complaining about his shoulder!

The Head Gardener's Son - Mr. Don Saunders

I was born in Bishops Lydeard in 1930 and started at the school when I was five. In those days Mr. Tipper, the headmaster, used the cane. I remember the first day I went up from the middle class we were outside doing Physical Training. We were all down on our haunches in four lines and the boy in the next line knocked my arm and made me slip. I knocked everyone back as I fell and was immediately told to go inside. Mr. Tipper came down, having put the cane up his sleeve, and told me to catch hold of the coat pegs and bend over. Bang, bang, bang - "You won't do that again, go and sit there until they come back."

Every other Monday we went on Wither's coach, which came from Bagborough, to Rowbarton in Taunton for woodwork. I also remember Mrs. Allen, who live in 9 Church Street, used to take us for sword dancing in Lynchfield House. We all had wooden swords, which at the end, we would clip together like a big star. Football was played on the field opposite Webbers in Taunton Road.

During the War we used to have exemption cards, something like 30 half days a year, from school to go up and work on the farms, for 6d an hour.

My dad, Arthur, was gardener at Dene Court for 35 years and became Head Gardener for Mr. T. C. Armitage, who bred race horses and greyhounds there. Dad used to open the greenhouse early in the morning and do the watering until late at night. As times were bit a hard between the wars, often on a Saturday dad would say. "What have we got for tomorrow then, mother?" She would reply. "Not a bit." So dad said. "Come on then, boy." Off we would go on our bikes to Dene Court.

"You take that there stick and go and shake them there stinging nettles." Out would come a pheasant or maybe a rabbit or hare and dad would shoot them. Back at home mother would pick away at the pheasant's feathers and throw them on the fire causing the whole room to smell. We had an old black range to cook on with two hobs and an oven.

My grandfather, William, like my father, was also born in the village. He lived down the lane in the cottage beside Swan Cottage. William was the village postman and met the mail train at 5.30 am to get the letters, which he took back to the Post Office in Gore Square for sorting. He used to walk up the village delivering letters and on to Cothelstone Manor, then across the fields to Cushuish and back to Toulton Farm. The last part of his round took him across the fields to Terhill and sometimes on to Bagborough.

I remember one unpleasant incident during the War. Mr. Merson used to bring his cattle down the village from his fields (now Darby Way Estate) to be milked at Lime Trees. One of the cows got into the churchyard through the little gate and ran all along the front to where the ground got higher and then tried to jump the railings. Unfortunately it got impaled and Hubert Webber, the butcher, had to get permission to shoot it. Later all the railings were removed as part of the war effort. Ernie Merson, when he didn't have cows up there, used to grow peas and we kids went up there to pick them and they were sold to Martin White from Kingston.

Mr. Merson opened a fish and chip shop, adjoining the Bird in Hand, for two or three years during the war. It was 9d for fish and chips. His daughter, Phyllis, sold ice cream in the summer from the front of Lime Trees.

Gwen Saunders recalls: *in 1950 I used to come to Bishops Lydeard to dances. We came in a coach from Curry Rivel with the band, Ray Roy's Band. I met Don at one of the dances and I shall always remember his brother saying. "Mother, I think you are going to have another ginger-haired daughter-in-law."*

Tiny Weaver was the policeman here then. He would stand no nonsense from anyone at a dance. Tiny would bang their heads together and take them out to stand against the wall at Warre House until the late bus came at midnight.

Gwen and Don married in 1953 and moved to Greenway when it was completed in 1958.

The Yeoman Farmer's wife - Mrs. Margaret Morris

Margaret was born at Willett Farm, which had been rented by her Uncle, Jack White, the England cricketer. Margaret's father had taken over the farm for some five or six years before going to Washford Farm. Margaret trained as a nurse and was nursing in Exeter for ten years. In 1967 she moved to Pound Farm after marrying Alan Morris.

The Morris family first came to the Parish in 1852 when William Morris took the tenancy of East Lydeard Farm with his family of nine - seven boys and two girls. John Morris was aged one when the family moved to East Lydeard Farm and Charles Morris was actually born there. In time, the older sons moved away into farming, mainly in West Somerset, and both the girls married into the Skinner family at Pound Farm.

John stayed at home and Charles went into engineering, first in Taunton and then on to Calcutta, building bridges and water pumps amongst other things and he became the senior partner at Jessops. On his return to England he had an office in London and bought a small estate at St Albans in Hertfordshire where he kept a pedigree herd of Devon cattle.

In 1913, when the Sandhill estate was sold, Charles bought East Lydeard Farm and his brother John had Conquest and Portman Farms, where he had moved with his mother. John's sister, Emma - the widow of Alfred Skinner - with her son, Gordon, bought Pound Farm.

Following a fire at Portman Farm, John Morris moved to Conquest Farm and married Amy Barrington of Creech St Michael. They had two sons, Jack and Alan. Amy became a founder member of the Mother's Union in Bishops Lydeard and played a leading role for many years. Jack inherited East Lydeard Farm from his Uncle Charles.

When John Morris died in 1925, Alan, then 16, and his mother continued to farm both Conquest and Portman Farms. In 1951 Alan sold Conquest Farm and bought Pound Farm from his cousin, Gordon Skinner - Gordon retiring to Warre Cottage now known as Frog House.

Gordon and his father Alfred, were Churchwardens at St Mary's Church for some 60 years.

It was recorded in the Parish Magazine : *a most gratifying incident in parochial life took place on Tuesday 27th November 1894 when Alfred Skinner was the recipient of a handsome gold watch, subscribed to by some sixty parishioners, in appreciation of his valuable services 'in all matters for the welfare of the parish'. Mr C.E.J. Esdaile in a most happy and kindly speech, asked Mr. Skinner to accept the watch as a token of the parishioners goodwill.*

The front pews in the Church were made of oak grown and seasoned at East Lydeard Farm and were placed there in memory of Gordon Skinner and Jack's eldest daughter - tragically killed in a riding accident.

1987 Alan Morris with the vicar the Rev. Lincoln-Jones.

Alan served for another 39 years as Churchwarden, after Gordon, which meant that the farmer from Pound Farm had been a Churchwarden for a hundred years.
Alan did a lot of hunting with the Harriers and walked puppies for the Fox Hounds. He was one of the original Trustees of the Village Hall. He died in May 1997 and on the 14th January 2001, the former Bishop of Crediton, the Rev. Peter Coleman, dedicated the new porch doors which had been installed in Alan's memory.

St Mary's Church porch doors in memory of Alan Morris.

Sir Arthur C Clarke's Brother - Mr. Fred Clarke

No reminiscences of Bishops Lydeard in the Twentieth Century would be complete without the inclusion of the Clarke Family. Fred's great grandfather, Charles Wright, was the postmaster as far back as 1860. The Post Office then was in Gore Square, built in 1842. On his death his wife, Julia, took over as postmistress - the same Julia Wright that Mrs. Eller recalled as a patient in Cotford Hospital in the early 1920's. Julia would have been about 100 at that time.

Julia's daughter, Elizabeth, was to marry Thomas Clarke who had arrived as a young man from Cambridgeshire to take up service with Sir Wroth Lethbridge, as coachman. Thomas built a new house, 2 Gore Square, in 1888 and this became the new Post Office. Later their eldest daughter, Florence Hepzibah, took over as the postmistress and continued for 35 years.

Fred Clarke takes up the story. *My mother, Nora, worked in a number of post offices including Minehead, where she was born, and Porlock, which was owned by her uncle. My father, Charles, the eldest son of Thomas Clarke, had been brought up in the Post Office at Bishops Lydeard. When, as the newly commissioned Lt. Charles Clarke in the Royal Engineers, he was walking with a friend in Taunton and the*

The house in Blenheim Road, Minehead, where Arthur and Fred were born. Their grandmother ran it as a guesthouse.

friend said. "That's a pretty girl," pointing to a young lady across the street. "That's the girl I'm going to marry," said Charles and crossed the road to introduce himself. They obviously had a lot in common from their backgrounds and got married, in Minehead, on 29th July 1915.

My maternal grandmother insisted that my mother leave London for Minehead to have her first child. Arthur duly arrived, early in the morning, on 16th December 1917. Later, in April 1921, I was to be born in the same house - 4 Blenheim Terrace (now 13 Blenheim Road), Minehead.

At the end of the War my father had wanted an outdoor life and was determined to buy a farm. Together with a friend, Donald, he bought the very run down Beetham Farm, near Chard. It was a disaster and mother and father lost a lot of money.

By some miracle the house that my grandmother, Elizabeth, always said she wanted to retire to, was vacant. Its name was Ballifants. My father wrote to Sir Dennis Boles asking him to support his application. Sir Dennis replied quickly - 'Ballifants is the house your mother loved and how happy she would be to see you there. All my influence will be for you.' So we arrived at Ballifants and mother immediately advertised in a London paper for paying guests, at 3 guineas a week for full board, in order to make ends meet.

Father had been wounded and ill several times during the War and his trouble began soon after we moved to Ballifants. Violent attacks of pain came suddenly and in less than a year he was practically an invalid. He finally died in the Bristol Infirmary in 1931 but not before his great joy, Mary, and last son, Michael, had been born.

Ballifants Farm.

I never remember, as a child, food being in short supply. We were largely self-sufficient with the large garden crowded with potatoes, cabbages, carrots, onions and parsnips, with plum, apple and pear trees sheltering the black and redcurrant bushes near the strawberry beds. Fresh meat came from Webbers. Mother had an arrangement with Mr. Webber. She would take one of her pigs to his shop and he would kill, skin and prepare it, keeping half for his trouble, and return the other half which was hung on large hooks at Ballifants to be used when required. Every Saturday Mr. Kilford would deliver our bread of a dozen loaves.

Harvesting had to be carried out by casual labour which was never paid for, but mother used to loan out her horses or implements, in exchange, to the farmer when he required them for his own crops. It was the job of us children to take the food into the fields, strong cheese and crusty bread with plenty of cider, which we made at Ballifants with our own apples.

Both Arthur and I went to school in Bishops Lydeard. As we got older we had to walk the mile long journey and at busy times, like lambing, we had to get ourselves dressed and breakfasted. This meant we rarely got to school on time and I remember Mr. Tipper caning me three times a week for being late! I don't remember much about school in Bishops Lydeard, although Arthur remembers, with great affection, Miss Hanks, later Mrs. Quelch, who died at the the great age of 99. I do remember a job we had to do which was cutting up sheets of newspaper into six inch squares. They were then tied at one corner into bundles of fifty and hung in the toilets!

Nora Clarke at Ballifants with her children Fred, Arthur, Mary and Michael.

Both Arthur and I went on to Huish Grammar School. I was always getting into trouble and took great care to keep out of my brother's way. It was here that he developed his passion for books and science. Michael also went to Huish and my sister, Mary, to Bishops Fox's School.

Arthur's scientific interests emerged at an early age. At one time he bought the parts for a crystal wireless. Essentially these were the crystal, like a small lump of sugar, a fine twisted steel wire, known as the cat's whisker, terminals and a coil of wire to connect everything together. He neatly screwed everything to a piece of wood, connected up a pair of earphones from an old telephone set, and triumphantly introduced Ballifants to Henry Hall! He enjoyed a steady income from crystal sets selling them for half a crown each.

I was always roped in to assist Arthur with his experiments. One Christmas he was given a chemistry set. The book of instructions was followed carefully and all the fascinating things to do with the strange liquids and powders were tried. We liked the noisy ones best and, borrowing a pestle and mortar from the kitchen, mixed together saltpeter, sulphur and carbon to make gunpowder. Eventually Arthur got the mixture right, after singeing our hair and eyebrows, and prepared for Guy Fawkes Day. The simple fireworks were quite spectacular but Arthur wanted upwards movement, so rockets were the next step. As they got bigger, more powerful and more dangerous, he began to add payloads. There were balsa wood wings to help them get back to earth and I was sent to the far end of the field to collect them. As the loads got heavier they barely left the ground and would explode about face level!

Arthur's interest in communications was stimulated by our Uncle George (Grimstone), he had married Aunt Floss (the postmistress). Being the engineer at Cotford Asylum he had helped Arthur with his crystal set. When the hospital

A young Sir Arthur C. Clarke in his study at Ballifants. His telescope can be seen in the background.

telephone system was converted to an automatic system, much of the pieces of equipment found there way to Ballifants. Soon a telephone system was installed from Arthur's bedroom to his study and I had to spend many hours listening into an earpiece which seemed to make less sound than came through the open window! When he decided to extend the system he used the barbed wire fences round the farm. These were often damaged by the cows and horses scratching against the posts at night and fault-finding took up more time than any used in talking on the system

To study space and the stars Arthur needed a telescope and we acquired an old field telescope - a relic from the Boer War. It was not very good, so with a book from the library, cardboard tubes and some lenses, Arthur made an efficient telescope which lasted years. On being given a Meccano set one Christmas he was able to build a stand for the telescope and the Meccano remained in that form for the rest of his childhood. The remainder of Sir Arthur C. Clarke's life is well documented. As for the rest of the family, I started my working life in the Taunton Post Office before the Second World War. After which I went to London for the next 30 years as a heating engineer before, like all good Somerset folk, returning to my roots to live at Dene Court. Mary trained as a nurse and Michael tilled the soil of Ballifants until his untimely death.

The Clarkes. Fred, Mary, Arthur and Michael.

and finally..........

The Many Faces of Bishops Lydeard

Village life has at its core the school, the church and its pubs, clubs and societies. The Dramatic Society productions and the Flower Show were just two of the longest running activities over the last century. Also celebrations have been staged to mark important events in village and national life and for many years the annual carnival was always a highlight for the village. The following pages record some of these events. The author has tried to name as many people as possible in the photographs but inevitably there are gaps. If anyone recognizes someone who is not named, the author would be pleased to hear from you.

One of the earliest school photographs, showing Mr Simons, the Headmaster and his wife on the left. Unknown date.

Schooldays

School photographs have been part of school life for the last hundred or so years. The photographs taken in the first decades of the twentieth century particularly show the fashions of the times.

The girls of the school in 1911

Back row: Edie Ellis (student teacher), Dorothy Matravers, Daisy Sedgbeer, ?, Florence Hawkins, ?, Poppy Simons, Majorie Saunders, Kitty Harris, Majorie Pavey, Miss Perry

Middle row: ?, Renee Jones, ?, Lucy Virgin, Rene Lock, Nelly Bellamy, Maggie Robbins, Annie Sully, Emilie Pope, Elsie Shattock, Winnie Hill, Lizzie Hobbs

First row: Elsie Simons, ?, Olive Lock, ?, ?, May Gooding, Lillie Lomand, ?, Lillian Saunders, Beatrice Bond, ?

Front: ?, Lillie Newick, Janet Blackmore, Joyce Blackmore, Ada Lock, Gladys Saunders (Palmer) aged 4, ? Simons, Lilian Bellamy

1926

Back row: Mr Tipper (Headteacher), George Gilfoy, Ted Gillard, Jim Binding, Reg Newick, Harold James, Eddie Knight, Fred Waygood, Cole, Norman

Middle row: Elsie Welch, ? Ward, Hiscocks, Joan Jobling, Miss Hanks, ?, Nesta Lock, ?, Iris Rose

First row: Walter Hitchcock, Lily Milton, ? Binding, Elsie Rodgers, Phyl Hitchcock, Marj Yandell, Florie Gardner, Gertie Bray, Gladys Bray, George Totterdell

Front: Roy Holcombe, ?, Geoff Heal, Leslie Hughes, Bill Perrot, Claud Snell, Bob Bellamy, Geoff Welsh, Reg Symons

1930

Back row:	George Knight	Sid Hobbs	Bert Withers	Stan Hughes		
2nd row:	Doreen Keirle	?	Mary Waygood	Glad Rosling	Clarice Snow	Gwen Kilford
3rd row:	Kath Barrington	Pat Lovell (Lathbury)	Mr Tipper	Ethel Shepherd	Edith Greenslade	
4th row:	Lorna Rich	Dolly Barker	Doris Boon	Nora ?	Edith Hancock	Lily Hoare
Sitting:	Jimmy Salter	Frank Branchflower	Geoff Keirle	Sid Howe	Bert Mann	

Mr. E. A. Wilcox became Headmaster after the retirement of Mr. Tipper. In 1949 he said the following about the school:

Times have changed very much since I was a boy at school. More is being done for children than ever before. The school caters for children from five to fifteen and meals are served daily to 175. Milk is also supplied in bottles. In work and play there is a competition among the four houses of the school. Brendons, Quantocks, Dene and Lydeard. A points system is allocated and the winning house, both in sports and work, has its name inscribed on the school shield. We hold a Sports Day each July. For the boys there is cricket in the summer and football in the winter is enjoyed on the adult ground (Taunton Road). Boxing in the hall in winter. The girls have netball, rounders and tennis according to the season while both boys and girls of the 14 plus group have a lesson each week in ballroom dancing. They also attend the Taunton swimming baths where over half of those attending have learned to swim this year. The Village Hall is used for physical culture in wet weather and also for rhythmic dancing, film strip projection and other activities.

Mr. E. A. Wilcox 1949

At that time physical culture was being taken by Mr. F. Roberts, a broad-shouldered ex-fighter pilot. He also took mixed classes for dancing lessons at the Village Hall.

Mr. Roberts: *It's a great help to young people to learn a little dancing before they leave school. It gives them an introduction to the dance hall, so that they won't feel self-concious when they are older. Before, young people who had not had the opportunity to dance seemed out of place, so they missed the being able to join in the fun at the village dance. Much of the social life of the village takes place in the Village Hall and the village dances are part of the life of the community and the dance lessons have helped a lot in the boys' and girls' social education.*

Above. Mr. Roberts taking a physical culture lesson.

Right. A dance lesson in the Village Hall. This dance was called 'The Maxina' and the music was provided by a gramophone.

The Choir c. 1925

Back row:											
?	Mr. Northcombe	Mr. Robbins	Fred Lovell	Percy Hanks	Bert Hughes	Bill Jones	Fred Stone ?	Mr. Saint	Thomas Lilley	Leonard Jones ?	Frank Hillier
Front row:											
Leslie Hughes	Charlie Waygood	Horace Yandell	?	Mr. Tipper	Reverend Fitch	Charlie Stone ?	?	Ralph Coleman	?	Fred Bestwetherick	

The Bellringers 1932

Left to right standing:
A. Baker F. Essex J. Scully A. Salter R. Stone R. Lock W. Welch
Left to right sitting:
R. Young F. Ames

Dramatic Society

The Society came into being in 1934 under the initiative of Mrs. Fitch, the vicar's wife, who wrote one act plays. The one acters were put on as part of Variety Evenings of entertainment. In 1937 the Rev. John Du Bulay Lance came and with Arthur Bicknell, as stage manager, launched into three act plays. 'Hobsons Choice' was the first full length play, performed in the school on planks laid on beer bottle cases! The following year the Society entered the Somerset Drama Festival and won the cup in the B Class with the play 'Pot Bound'.

Plays were put on during the war until 1941. Names to remember from the pre-war years were the Webber Family, Lovell, Keirle, Kilford and Lloyd Owen. Plays were restarted after the war in 1946 and in those early years the plays were always praised for the sturdily built and imaginative sets - Arthur Bicknell was the wizard stage manager until his death in 1951. Frank Lathbury took on the job and served the Society for the next thirty years.

Until 1960, the Society's Silver Jubilee, only one production a year had been put on, from then, until their final year in 1989, there were two a year. It was noted at their Golden Jubilee that Pat Lathbury had been involved in every production, in some capacity on stage, back stage and running the Box Office.

Pot Bound 1938

Left to right: Pat Lovell (Lathbury), Mrs Webber, Majorie Webber, Rhona Owen, Ulick Huntington, Doreen Keirle, Harold Kilford, Barbara Bradshaw, Harold Kilford, John Dury

The More the Merrier 1962

Standing: Beverley Bolton   Peter Dawson   Ken Webber   Pat Lathbury   Ulick Huntington

Sitting: Margaret Lyons   Gillian Lathbury   Liz Williams   Randall Hoyle

The back stage crew

Peter Hughes   Bob Pettit   Frank Lathbury   John Villis   Tony Brooks

When we are Married 1977

Standing:	Phil Tebb	Maggie Cooksley	Mervyn Clapp	Neil Harper	Chris Bramall	Tony Brooks	Clive Ross	Chris Collier	Kate Harwood
	Sitting:		Liz Williams	Anne Collier	Gaye Keating	Maralyn Bramall	Ann Pattemore		

Cricket

Cricket Team c. 1920

Games were then being played on Mr Armitage's field beside Dene Court

Standing:	Mr Tipper	Frank Hillier	Sam Burgess	Jack Fox	Leonard Saunders	?	?	Jack Sully	Mr Dury (Umpire)
Sitting:	Frank Sealy	Fred Heale	Bill Marshall	Mr Armitage	Raymond Lock	Jack Dury	?		

Scorer: Cyril Heale

President's Match 1990

At this game Mrs Ross (seated) dedicated the new pavilion, at the Cedar Falls Cricket Ground, in memory of her husband

Football

Football Team 1912

This was the first team to play for the newly formed Bishops Lydeard Football Club, founded by Captain Benson at Lydeard House in 1912.

Back row:	Jack Yandell	Tom Hartnell	?	?	?	?	George Lock	?	?	?	Mr Smith

Middle row:	Edgar Meade	Harry Holcombe	Mr Trickey	Captain Benson	Dr Frossard	Sam Burgess	?

Front row:	Cuthbert Saunders	Will Colman	?	?

Bishops Lydeard Football Team 1919 - 20

The Flower Show

On the August Bank Holiday of 1889 the first Flower Show was held at Lydeard House. There were entries from a wide area and the Williton Voluntary Band provided the music. The Show continued until 1912 and was revived for one event only, in 1920.

Twenty one years later, at Lynchfield House, a 'Dig for Victory' Show was held, raising £110 for the Red Cross. In 1946 the Flower Show moved to the Village Hall where it took place continuously until 2000.

These very successful shows were under the chairmanship of Mr. George Lee until his death in 1974 and then continued to flourish with the guidance of his son and daughter, Ray and Robin.

The Flower Show was revived yet again in 2003.

Flower Show 1974. Mr. Holley (sec.) Mr. George Lee, (chairman) shortly before his death, and Mr. Jack Bowyer (judge)

Flower Show 1982 Mrs. Iris Saunders with her grand-daughter, Helen Blows, showing the age range of competitors taking part in the show

Flower Show 1987

Mr Ray Lee (chairman) Miss Robin Lee (secretary) in the back row.

Committee members : Mr Ron Saunders (in the middle) and Mrs Gwen Saunders (far right).

Judges : Peter Fletcher Charlie Bond   Mrs Frances Osmant   Jack Bowyer.

Flower Show 2003
Cup Winners

Mrs Helen Newman Mr B. Norman Thea Sanders Samuel McDermot Mrs Mary Eaton Mr Richard Sanders

Dr Mark Anderson Mrs Jane Hinton June Harper and Adrian Flook MP and his wife Frangelica, who presented the cups.

Village Celebrations

The Village has always celebrated royal events such as Coronations and Jubilees. Also the end of both wars were marked by events in the Village. There were several annual events. Before the first war there was the annual Parish Walk which started and ended at Market Field, behind the Gore Inn, with teas and sports for the women and children and a beer tent for the men. The annual Ploughing Match always aroused great interest, the last of which was held at Conquest Farm on 31st October 1931. Attracting entries from a wide area was the annual Cothelstone Horse Show. Many arrived by train and walked up through the village to Cothelstone. The Friendly Societies each held their annual Church Parades starting from the Gore Inn. The oldest was the Tradesmens Friendly Society and the others were the Druids, Foresters and the Buffs.

The Bishops Lydeard Charter of 1291, granted by Edward I, permitted weekly markets on a Monday and two six day Fairs yearly. By 1875 the March Fair was still being held on the Friday before the last Saturday in the month for bullocks, horses and sheep. The September Fair was for 'all sorts of toys'. Within the following decade both Fairs had died out and the last of the wooden animal pens were removed from Market Field in 1940.

The Toy Fair was revived in 1942 and again in 1946 starting with an Opening Pageant, composed by Miss Frances Dunn. The original handwritten script still exists and goes as follows:

*(The players and stallholders are in the costumes of the eighteenth century.
The stallholders come along in groups from the Bell Inn talking and stand about at the top end of the stalls in Church Street.)*

BETSY: Well, Susan, we'm all ready now, and I do wish as how Mistress Lethbridge and Passon would come along and let us start away wi' it.
SUSAN: Aye and so do I, there's a fairin' or two I'd dearly love to lay hands on afore all they folks come along and sweeps un all up.
YOUNG TOM: (rushing round the corner from The Bell Inn) 'Ere's a stranger coming on 'orseback.
STRANGER: (riding through to Betsy and sweeping off his hat) Good day to you all. You seem in a very gay mood here in Lydeard. Pray tell me, someone, what is it all about.
BETSY: Well there now, fancy you not knowing that, Sir. Why 'tis Lydeard Toy Fair today.
SUSAN: I think you must ha' come from furrin parts, Lunnon or Wales or somewhere o' that, not to know about Lydeard Toy Fair.
STRANGER: Well, I don't you see, so you tell me all about it. Why do you have a Toy Fair and why today?
BETSY: Oh, it do go back a long ways, Sir, a very long ways.

SUSAN: (breathing in) Lor bless 'e Sir, it do go back so far as Edward the Second of England. 'E did grant this 'ere charter to Bishops Lydeard for to have a Horse and Cattle Fair on Lady Day, seein' as how our Church is St. Mary's.

BETSY: (looking towards the tower) And a grand old Church too.

STRANGER: (impatiently) But my good Dames, a Horse and Cattle Fair on Lady Day isn't a Toy Fair on the 8th September.

BETSY: We'm a coming to that Sir, we'm a coming to that.

SUSAN: It's like this 'ere Sir. They do say that the wimmen folk was fair crazy when they heard as how the men was goin' to have this 'ere Cattle Fair. "Do ye think" says they, "we can wear 'orses and cows around our necks or on top of our 'eads." They says, "We do want something purty like - fal-lals and gew gaws and such like for to buy. If you do have your Cattle Fair," says they, "we'll have our Toy Fair."

BETSY: So 'twas settled like and the wimmen says, "If you have your Fair Lady Day, we'll have ours on Our Lady's birthday - harvest should be over by about then and things settled down a bit, as the saying is."

SUSAN: And if you'll excuse me Sir, you seemingly a bit ignorant like, if you looks in your Prayer Book Calendar there you'll see it, 8th September, Nativity of the Virgin Mary.

BETSY: Have done Susan. (To the Stranger) And they wrote that 'ere charter out beautiful on parchment up to London Town, lawyers and that what could write, they did it and hung it all around wi' the Royal Seal and down it came, special messenger and all, and the Toy Fair was started.

STRANGER: Well, well, well.

SUSAN: And, oh Sir, if you did but know what a blessed thing it is, once a year, to buy wi'out having to ride to Taunton in a market cart all along with calves and pigs.

BETSY: Aye or pillion. If you could feel how hot my husband do get in summertime a'ridin on 'orseback, 'tes all right wintertime like sittin' beside kitchen fire.

SUSAN: And then you can't never get 'un to go to Taunton Town. Either 'tes the ploughing of hay-harvest or roots or someat.

CHILDREN: (rushing down church path) 'Ere comes Passon, 'ere comes Mistress Lethbridge - hurray, hurray - now we'll start the Toy Fair.

(Arrival of procession down the churchyard walk to the gate.)

MISTRESS LETHBRIDGE: Good neighbours all, wherever you come from, we, the folk of Lydeard, give you all a hearty welcome to our Toy Fair. We hope you will help us to clear the stalls and eat up what good things we have found you at Vine Cottage and repair to the garden at Lydeard House where you can enjoy the sports provided, or watch the tennis, or just wander where you will. And now I shall ask our good parson to open the Fair.

PARSON: According to the rights bestowed upon us by His Gracious Majesty King Edward the Second of England, I declare this Fair open and may God bless your pleasures.

Right. The village had six days of events to celebrate the return of the charter in 1981. Ulick Huntington played Edward II and Lavender Huntington, the Queen.

Below. The programmes for the Coronation festivities of 1911 and 1937.

Bishop's Lydeard & Cothelstone
CORONATION FESTIVITIES,
JUNE 22ND, 1911.
ORDER OF THE DAY'S PROCEEDINGS.

Peals from the Church Bells will be given at 6 a.m. and at intervals during the day.

Divine Service will be held at the Church at 11 a.m., and all who possibly can do so are asked to attend.

Procession. Immediately after Church Service the Band will play in the Church Square, and the Villagers are asked to assemble and fall in for a Procession through the Village. To specially mark this occasion, the Committee appeal for Decorated Bicycles and Cars, and Members of Friendly Societies will add to the effect by appearing in their Regalia. Street Decorations will also be appreciated.

Luncheon at 1.30 p.m. in a field at Cleeve Hill by the kind permission of P. S. Benson, Esq., and Mr. Chas. Saunders. Each holder of a ticket is asked to provide himself with a knife and fork, and CARVERS will please bring a carving knife and fork.

Drink Tickets are for use on the field during the day, and MINERALS may be had instead of Ale, if desired.

Children's Procession to start from the School at 3 p.m., and march to the Field.

Tea for Women and Children at 4.30 p.m. Each one is asked to provide a spoon.   **Dancing** during the Afternoon and Evening.

SPORTS.

The following programme will be arranged by the Sports' Committee:—

	1st Prize	2nd Prize	3rd Prize	4th Prize
Obstacle Race	5s.	3s.	2s.	
Bicycle Race for Men and Boys (Racing Bicycles Barred)	5s.	3s.	2s.	
Bicycle Race for Women	5s.	3s.	2s.	
Boot Race for Scouts	4s.	3s.	2s.	1s.
Obstacle Race for Scouts	4s.	3s.	2s.	1s.
Hat Trimming Competition for Men Competitors to be presented with the Trimmed Hats.	3s.	2s.	1s.	
Flat Race for Boys	3s.	2s.	1s.	
Flat Race for Girls	3s.	2s.	1s.	
Tug-of-War (eight men in a team)	One Pound.			
Half-mile Race (under 20 years)	5s.	3s.	2s.	
Quarter-mile Race (over 20 years)	5s.	3s.	2s.	
Egg and Spoon Race for Women	4s.	3s.	2s.	
Turk's Head Competition	3s.	2s.	1s.	
Fancy Get-up for Boys	4s.	3s.	2s.	
Fancy Get-up for Girls	4s.	3s.	2s.	
Flat Race for Women	4s.	3s.	2s.	
Decorated Perambulator or Mailcart, carrying a Baby	5s.	3s.	2s.	

This will be the First Competition.

The Committee confidently appeal to all to make the Coronation Day of King George V. a day of thorough amusement and enjoyment.

CHAS. E. J. ESDAILE, Chairman.
J. C. BADCOCK, Hon. Treasurer.
C. D. SIMONS, Hon. Secretary.

Printed at the "Somerset County Gazette" Office, Taunton.

Programme.
BISHOPS LYDEARD
Coronation Celebrations.
MAY 12TH. 1937.

2.30. OPEN-AIR SERVICE (see leaflet) in field West of Church.
British Legion, Boy Scouts, Girl Guides and Friendly Societies are asked to attend with Standards, Uniforms, Medals and Regalia.

3.0–4.30. SPORTS. See Page 2.

4.30–5.30. PICNIC TEA. See Page 3.

5.30. SPORTS.

8.0. BROADCASTING OF SPEECH by HIS MAJESTY THE KING.

9.0. BONFIRE and FIREWORKS
(Fireworks kindly presented by Lt.-Col. E. T. R. WICKHAM, M.V.O., M.P.)

SIDE-SHOWS, SKITTLING, DANCING.

Music will be provided during the afternoon and evening by
PEASEDOWN SILVER PRIZE BAND.

Beatrice Lady Boles has very kindly given a Coronation Mug for every child in the village and they will be presented by her in the Schools at 3.45 p.m., on Tuesday, May 11th, 1937.

Queen Elizabeth II Golden Jubilee 2002
The Jubilee was celebrated by eight days of events which culminated in a Jubilee Parade and Village Tea Party on the Village Green (above).

Seated on the dias are the Jubilee King, Ryan Venton, and Queen, Rebecca Locke with their attendants,
Amber Harley-Perks (left) and Jasmine Coles (right).
The Village Crier is Roger Sleap and seated is Florence Woollen who presented the prizes.

Top. On Sunday 29th October 2000, to commemmorate the Millenium, villagers planted 2000 bulbs at the entrance to the village off the A358.

The Carnival

1953

Left to right: Messrs. Player, Hodge, Sparks, Shattock, Sedgbeer, Shattock (T), Morris and Sturgess.

1968 Church Wives Group
Mrs. Martin, Val Burnett, Don Saunders, June Harper, Sylvia Steer, Gwen Saunders, Jean Huntington, Joyce Dekkers,
Chris Hughes.
Eddy Searles, John Dekkers.

1987
The Carnival took place each year for some four decades. The floats were originally towed by tractor but got bigger and bigger each year. Eventually the Carnival had to be stopped, for safety reasons, the lorries were too big to negotiate the village. The above photographs record the last Carnival, the Majorettes turning into Hither Mead and the Royal British Legion float - Oranges and Lemons.

The Doctors

| **Standing:** | Dr. Simon Harrison, | Dr. Rianne Sewell, | Dr. Roger Crabtree |
| **Seated:** | Dr. Philip Woodgate-Jones, | Dr. Tim Woodgate-Jones, | Dr. Richard Harrison. |